# OUR FRIEND JAMES JOYCE

# OUR FRIEND JAMES JOYCE

BY

## MARY AND PADRAIC COLUM

GLOUCESTER, MASS.

PETER SMITH

1968

ACKNOWLEDGMENTS

Five lines from the poem "To Ireland in the Coming Times" from COLLECTED POEMS OF W. B. YEATS. Copyright 1906 by The Macmillan Company. Reprinted by permission of Mrs. Yeats, The Macmillan Company, New York and The Macmillan Company of Canada.

The quotations from poems, FINNEGANS WAKE, and A PORTRAIT OF THE ARTIST AS A YOUNG MAN are included with the permission of The Viking Press, Inc., who also, along with Faber & Faber, Ltd., granted permission for the use of excerpts from the LETTERS OF JAMES JOYCE.

Two unpublished letters by James Joyce and one unpublished letter by Nora Joyce. Reprinted by permission of The Society of Authors, as the Literary Representatives of the James Joyce Estate.

Excerpts from COLLECTED POEMS OF AE reprinted by permission of Macmillan & Company, Ltd., St. Martin's Press and Diarmuid Russell.

Several lines of poetry by Oliver St. John Gogarty. Reprinted by permission of the author's son, Oliver D. Gogarty.

*60,118*

# CONTENTS

The inspiration for *Our Friend James Joyce* came from Mary Colum, and the shape of the narrative was planned by her. Illness prevented her from writing as many of the chapters as she intended; however, by discussing the whole work with me, by recalling situations, by enlivening the recollections that we both could draw on, she, to a large extent, carried through what she initiated. . . . She wrote on sheets that were inscribed with the first line of a sonnet she loved, and that line which so expressed her should have a place here:

*Le vierge, le vivace at le bel aujourd'hui.*

P. C.

# I.  DUBLIN

# I.  PADRAIC COLUM

Dublin is a small city, so small that one can walk from the center to the outskirts in twenty minutes. It is a city that is commercial and bureaucratic and not industrial; little business of an absorbing nature is transacted there, and the citizens are leisurely in their ways and disengaged in their minds. The size of the city and the pursuits of the inhabitants give rise to an interest in character—an interest that was present in all the coteries that the Dublin of the turn of the century composed itself into. A "character's" doings and sayings would be repeated from coterie to coterie, losing nothing in drama or humor in the repetition. When I first met James Joyce, in 1901 or early in 1902, he was beginning to emerge as a Dublin "character." Already there was a legend about him.

That first meeting took place at one of Lady Gregory's evening parties. Seated in a corner were two young men whom I, who was about their age but had not been at the university, sized up as students. Now in Dublin at that time students (they were mostly male) were thought of somewhat as they were in medieval times, as knowledgeable, profane, and, to a certain extent, detrimental; my recognizing the two young men as such implied all that. But these two were obviously not the ordinary run of students, since they were in a company (it would have been more fitting to say "congregation") that included Lady Gregory and William Butler Yeats. Introduced to the two, I found I had heard their names before: they were Oliver Gogarty and James Joyce.

Each was already something of a celebrity. Oliver Gogarty, then a student at Trinity College, was known as an athlete— a bicyclist and a swimmer—as well as one to whom many of the scandalously witty sayings that were going the rounds of Dublin were attributed. The other's distinction was much less general. A year or two before that, when he was not much more than eighteen, James Joyce had achieved something that would have been gratifying to a writer twice his age: he had had an article published in the important *Fortnightly Review.* It was a review of Ibsen's *When We Dead Awaken,* for which the playwright, at that time the great master of European drama, later had William Archer, his English translator, express his appreciation to the young critic. It was a creditable article, one that showed erudition, loftiness of outlook, and, as one who read it thoughtfully could see, a dedication.

Then, in 1901, in the bookshops had appeared a two-penny pamphlet by Francis Skeffington and James A. Joyce. Skeffington was an ardent advocate of equal rights for women, and his half of the pamphlet, entitled "A Forgotten Aspect of the University Question," dealt with the status of women in the Irish universities; Joyce's half, an attack on the projected National Theatre, bore the title "The Day of the Rabblement." That scornful title, very noticeable on the cover below Skeffington's sedate one, was well remembered by many who had no use for the pamphleteering of a pair of students who, by joining forces, had halved the cost to each of having their polemics printed. Joyce's text denounced the provincialism of the Irish project and demanded that its initiators make themselves into Europeans by producing certain of Ibsen's, Strindberg's, Hauptmann's, and Tolstoi's plays. Even these names were not mentioned with any adoration, however: readers were told of Strindberg's "hysterical power." How very assured this University College student was!

Yet, for all his scorn and assurance, here sat the pamphleteer, meekly taking tea or sherry and listening to Yeats and Lady Gregory discuss possible plays, possible productions, with the other guests, who were mostly members of the company of the National Theatre. I do not remember that Joyce entered the conversation that evening. He and Gogarty sat apart, near the door, as if they did not quite belong at the gathering.

It may have been on this occasion that Lady Gregory asked Joyce to "write something for our little theatre." It was a request that the young author of "The Day of the Rabblement" was often to be derisive about. I don't know whether it was Joyce or Gogarty who made up the limerick that is frequently quoted as Joyce's:

> There was an old lady named Gregory
> Who cried: "Come, all ye poets in beggary."
> But she found her imprudence
> When hundreds of students
> Cried: "We're in that noble category."

## MARY M. COLUM

The first I heard of James Joyce was under odd circumstances. I was living in a university residence house in Dublin, studying for the matriculation examination. It happened that one of the girl students in the house—a graduate, I seem to remember—got a postcard from one of the men students that annoyed her very much by its contents. At that time, though Queen Victoria was dead, girls took offense in Ireland at any uncalled-for communication or approach from the male sex. The contents of the postcard became known to a number of us younger girls: the writer, I remember, suggested a meeting or rendezvous of some sort; the signature was "James A. Joyce."

The recipient of the postcard seemed to know who the writer was, for, highly indignant, she penned a haughty answer that was meant to humiliate and insult this James A. Joyce. In due time she received an equally haughty reply, phrased with extreme politeness but conveying to her that it was foolish to imagine that he, James A. Joyce, would have perpetrated such a missive, as he never remembered to have seen her, and anyhow never communicated with girl students unless they were family friends. The extreme hauteur of the reply revealed to our minds a personality of such arrogance that we all, in the wisdom of our youth, agreed that Joyce was no gentleman to write to a lady in that strain. It would have been enough, we thought, for him to explain that another student had used his name: there was no resemblance between the handwriting on the postcard and that in the second communication.

Some time afterward I had my first glimpse of James Joyce: he was pointed out to me in Kildare Street, where the National Library was. My companion remarked, "There is James Joyce, the great genius of University College in his own estimation." He had already taken his B.A. degree, I was told, and in modern languages as if he were a girl student, for the girls at this time were supposed to be specialists in modern languages and literature, while the boys' domain was classics, mathematics, and similar masculine pursuits. Neither this information nor the appearance of James Joyce was engaging, and the odd rumors we heard about him at the time were very shocking to our youth and naïveté. He had given up religion, it was said, and went in for evil frequentations of all kinds. (I may say that, though a few of the worst and most dangerous male gossips I have ever known flourished in the city by the Liffey, on the whole I believe that the reputation of Dublin for gossip is largely unfounded. It is not really so gossipy as New York or London or Paris; though what gossip went on when I lived there was venomous enough.)

Male and female students at the university in those days paid little attention to one another, as such relations were frowned on by the authorities; though a girl student might speak to a brother who was a student, she did so only on special occasions. Marriages between students or former students were rare, though not exactly unknown. Later, when it was bruited that Joyce had eloped romantically to the Continent, we knew it could not have been with a girl student. We also heard that, unlike a boon companion of his who had brazenly married for money, Joyce had chosen a sweetheart who had not a penny—who had, in fact, worked for a living in a hotel.

Years later, when I came to know him well, Joyce was surprised at how little I had heard about him at the university, particularly from the students who gathered in the National Library. I did not tell him that my most marked recollection of him was that of seeing his name on a notice board for the nonpayment of certain fees. I knew nothing at the time of his family's straits.

Joyce and I were educated in the same way—an education typical of that which the middle and professional classes received in the Ireland of those days. Each of us was sent first to a series of private schools, primary and secondary, that the government had some control over and gave some subsidies to. A great feature of these schools, at the Intermediate (or secondary) level, were the competitive examinations, at which prize pupils could win awards of considerable sums of money. The award for the Junior Grade examination, covering three years, was twenty pounds (the sum was then worth about three times its present value); for the Middle Grade, covering two years, it was thirty pounds; and for the Senior Grade of one year it was fifty pounds. The Irish newspapers treated the Intermediate as well as the university examinations like horse races or prize fights, giving much publicity to the competition between Catholic and Protestant schools as well as to those between the various schools within each religion, and to the grooming of boys and girls for national championships. Joyce, who won several awards, was one of the scholastic champions of his day.

If one passed the tough Senior Grade examination at the Intermediate level, one was eligible to be inscribed as a matriculation student at a university. But there the examinations continued: one studied a year before taking a matriculation examination, after which came First Arts, Second Arts, and B.A. examinations, and, if one went farther, M.A. examinations.

Joyce and I both matriculated at what was then called the Royal University. It was the successor to the university Cardinal Newman projected, but was nonsectarian—not a Catholic university, that is, though one of its colleges, University College, which Joyce attended, was Catholic. Later the Royal University became the National University. Joyce had his degree from the Royal; I, coming after him, had mine from the National University.

I have often heard the Royal University spoken of disparagingly on the ground that it was not residential, as Dublin University (Trinity College) is. Actually the Royal turned out some of the best educated people I have ever known. It did not give a practical or pragmatic education, but it succeeded in producing cultivated and even learned persons, of whom Joyce was one.

## II.  PADRAIC COLUM

James Joyce lived on the north side of Dublin—north of the river, that is. In a city so small, this fact would not appear to have much significance. But in Dublin opinion it had: the north side was a little less and the south side a little more bourgeois. Though his family had lived in various neighborhoods, at the time of our meeting, Joyce was a north-side man, as was Mr. Bloom. For the few years I had been in the city I had lived on the south side, and Joyce to me was a man of another town.

Several times after we were introduced at Lady Gregory's, he and I came within recognizing distance on the street or in the National Library, but we had no communication. Joyce was aloof, and his blue eyes, perhaps because of defective vision, seemed intolerant of approach. He would enter the rotunda of the reading room at the library generally between eight and nine o'clock in the evening. I won't say that he entered arrogantly, but he entered as one who was going to hold himself aloof from the collectivity there. I was not interested in what he was reading, but once when I came to the counter after he had been there, an attendant said of a book that had been put aside, apparently to be reserved, "For Mr. Joyce." It was a book on heraldry.

The time came when I did make an advance to Joyce, however: the gesture was prompted by his transitory presence in a circle I belonged to.

The patron of the younger poets—one might say the promoter of poetry—in the Dublin of that day was "AE," George William Russell. Poet, painter, theosophist, and man of great heart, AE had gathered a group 'round him that met at his house on Sunday evenings to discuss recently published or about-to-be published work and to adumbrate the shape of the coming Irish literature. He had already collected and brought to publication poems of certain poets in their twen-

ties, of whom I was one. (Looked back on, this seems an act
of practical benevolence.) Well, I was told that Joyce—not,
of course, as one of the group—had gone, manuscript in hand,
to AE's house, and there had been a colloquy. The encounter,
like all events affecting the literati, was well dramatized by
its retailers. "I do not know whether you are a fountain or a
cistern," AE was reported to have said to him. And, on reading
his poems, "I do not think you have chaos enough in you to
make a world."

Joyce and I being of the same age, my name, it appeared,
had come into AE's discourse with him. I felt the confrontation as a challenge. "What sort of poetry does he write?" I
asked my informant. "Oh, like yours—subjective-objective
lyrics," was the inaccurate reply.

Now that Joyce had come upon my terrain, it was proper
that I should measure myself with him: this I decided one
evening as we passed each other in the library. As he went
through the turnstile on his way out, I went through too and
spoke to him on the stairway.

I think he took my approach as an act of homage (it was)
and was willing to go along with me conversationally. We went
out on Kildare Street and kept walking on, then along O'Connell Street until we turned toward where he lived. By this
time Joyce was talking personally, or perhaps I should say bio-
graphically.

Looking back on that promenade, I know that I could have
had no better introduction to the personality and the mind of
that unique young man. He talked, perhaps, as a formed person talking to one whom he suspected of being unformed; he
delivered, as he often did in those days, some set speeches.
What maturity he had then!

The event that had occasioned the meeting was soon dismissed by him, for the largeness of AE seemed to him a vacu-
ity. Considering the scholasticism of one and the neopaganism
of the other, their conjunction for even an afternoon was mysterious. The other poet of our town Joyce put on a different
plane. "Yeats has written what is literature—even what is
poetry," he said and then spoke of one of his stories, "The
Adoration of the Magi." For the new nationalist movement,

the Gaelic League, he had no regard. "I distrust all enthusiasms," he said.

It was natural to think, and I suppose I thought it, that a
young man who distrusted all enthusiasms was a singular character. And for Joyce to say this in the Dublin of the day was
to set himself up as a heretic or a schismatic, one who rifles
the deposit of the faith. "And if history and the living present
fail us, do there not lie hid among those spear-heads and
golden collars over the way in the New Museum, suggestions
of that age before history when the art, legends and wild my-
thology of earliest Ireland rose out of the void? There alone is
enough of the stuff that dreams are made of to keep us busy
a thousand years." So Yeats had written, at the age that Joyce
was then. To us at that time, belonging to "a movement"
meant fellowship, exhilaration. It meant moving away from
the despondency of the generation before and toward a new
national glory. Who would not be in such a movement? And
it was animated by enthusiasm.

I am trying to find a word for the way the young man standing on that street corner said, "I distrust all enthusiasms."
It was not with any youthful bravado. It was rather like one
giving a single veto after a tiring argument.

On the same street corner Joyce spoke of his family in a
way that did not take from the dignity of the part he was
playing that evening. And what was that part? Of a mentor,
perhaps. Joyce was a solitary in his thought, but he was pleased
to have a disciple. It may have been necessary for him to show
part of his life to that possible disciple. Anyway, on that occasion he showed himself as the scion of an outstanding family.
His father, who had come to Dublin from Cork, had had a
sinecure; he had lost it and got through his capital in practices
of good fellowship. Joyce permitted himself to be a little
homiletic: "What I kept, I lost; what I gave, I have. If my
father was able to say that he need not regret what he has
come to."

Joyce's father, John Stanislaus Joyce, was well known in the
Dublin bars, the restaurants, and the race courses; he had the
sort of status in the city that a man who has frittered away
his prospects in the name of good fellowship can have in any

easygoing social milieu. He had a good voice and would sit down at the piano in a public place and rattle off a tune, sing a traditional song or an air from an opera. About the time I first met James Joyce a characteristic story was going the rounds about John Stanislaus. It begins in the rain as he and a crony are mounting a jaunting car to go to the races. John Stanislaus curses. The crony, a pious man, reproves him: "Don't you know that God could drown the world, John?" "He could if he wanted to make a bloody fool of himself." The comedy of the story was in the unctuous voice of one and the barking voice of the other.

But it is not Joyce as the young man who separated himself from the rest of us, nor Joyce as the son of a Dublin personage, that I remember from that fortunate evening; rather it is Joyce as the maker of beautifully wrought poems. A poet in those days was expected to know his own poems and be willing to deliver them. I had heard AE, swinging from vowel to vowel, chant:

> *Its edges foam'd with amethyst and rose,*
> *Withers once more the old blue flower of day.*

And I had heard Yeats make actual enchantment out of:

> *O colleens, kneeling by the altar-rails long hence,*
> *When songs I wove for my beloved hide the prayer.*

Joyce spoke his verse with deliberateness and precision, but in a naturally beautiful voice that had been cultivated for singing. The effect was more personal than in the case of AE or Yeats; it was Joyce exalted into the mode in which he knew himself free:

> *What counsel has the hooded moon*
> *Put in thy heart, my shyly sweet,*
> *Of love in ancient plenilune,*
> *Glory and stars beneath his feet—*
> *A sage that is but kith and kin*
> *With the comedian Capuchin?*

*Believe me rather that am wise*
*In disregard of the divine,*
*A glory kindles in those eyes,*
*Trembles to starlight. Mine, O Mine!*
*No more be tears in moon or mist*
*For thee, sweet sentimentalist.*

"The simple liberation of a rhythm": this was his definition
of the lyric at the time. I shall always remember his rendering
of lyrics that were favorites with him then—a rendering without the lilt that Irish poets are apt to give the verse they are
repeating, one in which the poem became stylized speech
(but with exceptional beauty of voice). I recall his reading
of Ben Jonson's:

*Still to be neat, still to be drest,*
*As you were going to a feast;*
*Still to be powder'd, still perfumed:*
*Lady, it is to be presumed,*
*Though art's hid causes are not found,*
*All is not sweet, all is not sound.*

*Give me a look, give me a face*
*That makes simplicity a grace;*
*Robes loosely flowing, hair as free:*
*Such sweet neglect more taketh me*
*Than all th' adulteries of art;*
*They strike mine eyes, but not my heart.*

I shall remember, too, his rendering of Beatrice's song in the
last act of *The Cenci*—"False friend, wilt thou smile or
weep / When my life is laid asleep?" And a lyric of Mangan
which even that poet's most devoted readers have passed over,
became memorable when repeated by Joyce:

*Veil not thy mirror, sweet Amine,*
*Till night shall also veil each star!*
*Thou seest a twofold marvel there:*
*The only face so fair as thine,*
*The only eyes that, near or far,*
*Can gaze on thine without despair.*

It was sometime in the spring of 1902, whether before or after our meeting I do not recall, that Joyce stood on a platform before the Literary and Historical Society of University College to deliver an address on James Clarence Mangan. Fellow students who heard him said he was as composed and dignified as any young man could be. And yet these same students had heard him tell of his seedy adventures and, altering that persuasive voice of his into a raucous one, repeat verses of his own composition that were scandalous. The poet he spoke about had been claimed as an exemplar by Yeats:

> *Nor may I less be counted one*
> *With Mangan, Davis, Ferguson . . .*
> *True brother of a company*
> *That sang, to sweeten Ireland's wrong,*
> *Ballad and story, rann and song.*

Mangan was praised by the youthful Joyce, not for his allegiance to the national idea, but for his artistry, and he mentioned four or five poems that were to please him to the end of his days.

The address, which was published in *St. Stephen's*, the college magazine, in May of 1902, is less an essay on Mangan than an imaginary portrait—a portrait doubtless influenced by Pater's approach and style. In it there is wisdom and there is music. The student, then barely twenty, shows wisdom when he declares that "Poetry, even when apparently most fantastic, is always a revolt against artifice, a revolt, in a sense, against actuality." There is music throughout the address, as there was from the first, not only in the poems of *Chamber Music*, but in all of Joyce's writing. And the note of dedication that was in his article on Ibsen is heard again in some passages: "Finally, it must be asked concerning every artist how he is in relation to the highest knowledge and to those laws which do not take holiday because men and times forget them. This is not to look for a message but to approach the temper which has made the work, an old woman praying, or a young man fastening his shoe, and to see what is there well done and how much it signifies."

To regard Joyce's address on Mangan as just another, but an exceptionally thoughtful and imaginative, speech by a student ambitious for a hearing by the Literary and Historical Society would be a misconception. Delivered, as C. P. Curran recalls, in a tone "metallic in its clearness and very deliberate, as if coming from some old and distant oracle," the address was— as Joyce intended it to be—an event in the literary history of his time. The students who were present did not recognize it as an event, naturally enough. Dr. Felix Hackett[1] tells us that "The paper tried its audience very hard. A symphony can scarcely be appreciated at a first hearing." As soon as Joyce had finished, the tension he had imposed was dissipated. The discussion that followed was of the ordinary kind, the usual platitudes being uttered. "Acknowledging the vote of thanks," Dr. Hackett recalls, "Joyce made the defiant prophecy associated with Disraeli of a time coming when he would be heard."

And there was one person there who perhaps had a notion of the significance of the address: the chair was occupied by Dr. William Magennis, who as an Intermediate examiner had awarded the schoolboy Joyce two first prizes in English composition.

---

[1] Dr. Hackett, a classmate of Joyce who heard him give the address, has evoked that memorable occasion in the *Centenary History* of the Literary and Historical Society: "Beginning with the basic tones of romanticism and classicism, the first movement rose to a discussion of the judgement of the artist in relation to 'the highest knowledge'. . . . The second movement dealt with Mangan the man. The third movement, considering Mangan the writer, was an arabesque of language interwoven with rhythmic phrases from the verses of Mangan's Oriental dreamland. . . . This movement concluded with an eloquent passage echoing the phrase at the head of the printed essay: 'a memorial I would have . . . a constant presence with those that love me,' recalling the preoccupation of Mangan with death and the Orient. . . . The final movement returned to the highest abstractions about poetry in relation to the mournful verses of Mangan, with a finale beginning 'Beauty, the splendour of truth, is a gracious presence when the imagination contemplates intensely the truth of its own being or the visible world, and the spirit which proceeds out of truth and beauty is the holy spirit of joy'; and then soaring to a conclusion of musical and oracular utterance."

## III.  PADRAIC COLUM

The modern buildings that flanked the ducal residence, Leinster House—the National Museum on the right as one came through the gate in quiet Kildare Street, and the National Library on the left, with Leinster Lawn between—had only been in existence a generation at the time I met Joyce. It was probably in the National Library that the young Yeats, filled with enthusiasm for the auspices, wrote the lines I have quoted about the museum across the way: "There alone is the stuff that dreams are made of to keep us busy a thousand years."

Young people have no aptitude for evaluating what is theirs by inheritance; they step into it—that is all they know about it. So it was with the students and the casual intellectuals among the youth of Dublin. In the reading room of the National Library they had a handsome place in which to read, to view each other, to converse in the portico below, to make the encounters that permitted couples to walk together to their quarters. The library thus provided something of a social life as well as an intellectual life. It was hospitable. In the reading room, which was open until ten o'clock, could be seen the glamour-girl students as well as the notable young men. At that time the place was more frequented by young people than at present, for then the students of University College did much of their reading there; students today read in the libraries of their own universities.

Near the exit turnstile, in the reading room, was the counter at which one applied for books; on it were displayed recently published volumes. Behind this counter were attendants, scholarly men among them. The librarians had their offices along a corridor one entered from behind the counter.

But to speak of the trio in those offices, Mr. Lyster, Mr. Magee, and Mr. Best, as mere officials is not to do justice to them. They were personages in the intellectual life of Dublin, and have all three been transported into literature—one of them twice transported, for Magee is a character in George Moore's *Hail and Farewell* as well as in James Joyce's *Ulysses*.

The head librarian, Mr. Lyster, was about fifty in 1902. I remember someone saying, "It's strange that we use the word 'uncouth' but never the word 'couth.'" "And who would you say was 'couth'?" "I would say Mr. Lyster." He had a closely cropped beard, rather liquid eyes, and a rich, one might even say an unctuous, voice. One would scarcely be right to say he was voluble—it is hard to associate volubility with such a presence as Mr. Lyster's—but he was copious with his good speech. He was given to interrogatory openings: "May we not . . . ?" It would be going too far, again, to say he buttonholed one, but he did come close and he had a way of securing one's attention. "Is it not a Sahara?" I once overheard him say, enunciating every syllable, to a friend whom he was awakening to the vista of O'Connell Street, which apparently then and there had become unbearable to him. Fountains should be playing, it seemed, where statues stood in dreadful impassivity. Mr. Lyster was urging his friend to intercede with some wealthy Dublin family to provide the fountains.

I remember his speaking to me on one or two occasions, outside the counter of the reading room. Once, taking me to shelves that held many editions of *Faust*, he supplicated me to learn German so that I might read "the greatest projection of poetry since *Hamlet*." His address was very moving.

Mr. Lyster had made the pilgrimage to Tolstoi, John Butler Yeats told me. I believe he belonged to the elder Yeats' circle, which also included Edward Dowden. With Dowden and with Lyster's colleague Magee there would have been Goethean radiations; also, I think—but Dowden would not have liked this—a flavor of Matthew Arnold. Mr. Magee was religiously Wordsworthian. So the culture of the inner precinct was Goethean, Wordsworthian, and Matthew Arnoldish.

The head librarian was fond of repeating amorous verse, and when as an elderly gentleman he became engaged to a young lady he took me aside for the purpose of saying, "And has not our admired poet given us:

"I *would that we were, my beloved, white birds on the*
   *foam of the sea!"*

and going on, every syllable enunciated, down to:

"*Soon far from the rose and the lily and the fret of the flames*
   *would we be*
*Were we only white birds, my beloved, buoyed up on the*
   *foam of the sea.*"

I cannot now recall the incident that led up to his repeating
to me in a corridor of the library a verse from one of the Sufi
poets, in Emerson's version (at least I think it is Emerson's,
but I cannot find it in any collection)—the mystic contrasting
his esoteric freedoms with the rigidity of the pietist's external
devotion:

> *Thine is*
> *Spare fasts and orisons,*
> *But mine the wine of the inner shrine*
> *And sweet chase of the nuns.*

"When I repeated this most revealing verse to the Archbishop,
he did not assent at all," said Mr. Lyster. I really wondered if
the Quaker librarian wasn't having a little fun. Dublin's two
archbishops, the Catholic Dr. Walsh and the Protestant Dr.
Peacock, attended meetings as trustees of the National Library. It was the Catholic archbishop, of course, who had been
the recipient of the verse. "And sweet chase of the nuns" must
have been very appealing to the Most Reverend Dr. Walsh.

My first impression of W. K. Magee, the librarian whose
essays, bearing the pen name "John Eglinton," were among the
few contributions in that form to the nationalist literary movement, was one of shyness. He listened silently and, it seemed,
with embarrassment to some explanation about a book. He
was low-sized, with a fine head; his thoughtfulness was expressed in brown eyes. The eyes were remarkable: they gave an
impression of quietude, but I could imagine a flash coming
into them. He did not talk much—not by Dublin standards—
and yet men who relished conversation, George Moore and
Stephen MacKenna, found his companionship enjoyable.

As far as I remember, Mr. Magee's conversational way was

to affirm some point and let you talk 'round it. He too was a Goethean and, as I have said, a Wordsworthian: also, via Emerson, I imagine, a bit of an Oriental. These winds of doctrine had sifted down his original deposit of Calvinism, but there was enough of that left to make him ironic toward the proponents of an Irish nationalism that, as it seemed to him, would obviously eventuate in a Catholic state—and a Catholic state that would not have the internal opposition that had grown up along with European Catholic states. Mr. Magee had been marched into the ranks of the Irish Revivalists by that domineering recruiting officer, William Butler Yeats, and he must frequently have been perplexed by the combativeness of certain Protestant officers. He made a halting confession of faith, but his acceptance had none of the ardor shown by his fellow Ultonian, AE, even in the latter's repudiation of certain nationalist dogmas. AE made the things he repudiated seem exciting:

> "We are less children of this clime
> Than of some nation yet unborn
> Or empire in the womb of time.
> We hold the Ireland in the heart
> More than the land our eyes have seen,
> And love the goal for which we start
> More than the tale of what has been."

To John Eglinton "the tale of what has been" probably seemed an invention of Standish O'Grady.

Mr. Magee's Ulster Scots upbringing gave him a remove from which he could criticize expressions of exclusive nationalism. But I doubt if anyone ever heard the man—the librarian or the essayist—say an unfair, let alone a rancorous, word. It was this attractive and aloof, this distantly companionable, rather estranged person, whom certain of the wits of Dublin cast in the role of a drum-beating Orangeman, a dirk-using Border raider, a Bible-guided Covenanter. Was he aware of the casting? I do not know. But if he had heard of himself as a "filibustering fillibeg," his brown eyes would have opened wide in astonishment and he would have shaken his head over the Dubliners' strange japes.

Mr. Best was the youngest of the triumvirate of the National Library. He was more Continental than either Mr. Lyster or Mr. Magee, having studied in Paris. He had also, I am almost certain, been in Germany, for he was a philologist specializing in Old and Middle Irish, and the country of Thurneysen, Windisch, and Zimmer—names he spoke with the utmost reverence—was the second home (perhaps one should say the original home) of Celticists; if you had a yearning to know about the infixed pronoun, you would at that time have had to go to some scholar in Germany. Moreover, the great philologist, Kuno Meyer, seemed to be particularly attached to Mr. Best; George Moore complained that to get that most interesting of scholars to his house he had to work through Mr. Best, who was not at all sure that Kuno Meyer could spare the time while in Dublin for such marginal interests as George Moore's.

There was something of freshness about Mr. Best—of bloom, brightness. He was tall, blond, ruddy-complexioned, and wore particularly shining glasses. I have associated Mr. Lyster and Mr. Magee with the world of Goethe. Mr. Best suggested that world too, but in a different way: he was not, as far as I knew, a depository of Goethean wisdom, but he recalled one of those fresh, rather princely figures who, with a fund of enthusiasm, attended the aging Goethe, noting down his conversation, finding and assembling his early poems. Scholarly, enthusiastic, sociable, with a feeling for character and the ability to project it, Mr. Best was and is a delightful conversationalist.

## IV.  PADRAIC COLUM

After my first talk with him, leaving the National Library, I did not see Joyce for some time. He left Dublin for Paris in the fall of 1902, stopping over in London to get some reviewing to do—the normal way for a young Dublin man of letters to cash in on his bookishness. Yeats was in London then and helped Joyce with introductions to editors.

The story about that London visit that came back to Dublin

was concerned with the characters of Yeats and Joyce. Yeats is supposed to have said: "Joyce, the Japanese have a proverb: Be brave in battle, be truthful to your friends, be courteous always. You are not courteous, Joyce. After I introduced you to Arthur Symons and he entered into conversation with you you laughed." "Of course I laughed," Joyce replied. "He mentioned Balzac." But this is the Gogartian Joyce—"Kinch the knifeblade"—I later came to know; the Joyce who would have gone 'round with Yeats in London *was* courteous.

Joyce was away from Dublin for some months; then I heard that he had returned and later that his mother had died. I wrote a note of sympathy and received a formal acknowledgment. My family name has variant spellings, and when I wrote the note I used the one with the horrible "b" at the end, a form that a grandparent quite mistakenly had used. The next time I saw Joyce he was standing despondently where there was a small company. In a distant way he said, "I had a letter from you—or can it be there are two doves?" (In Latin, Irish, and French my name means that.) I mentioned the variations in spelling. "And which do you use when your singing robes are about you?"

This was Joyce at his most detached. All of us used the cold approach from time to time, of course—the "frozen mitt" was often proffered. Still, Joyce's attitude of ironic detachment toward me was not surprising. The nationalist group around *The United Irishman,* with which I was associated, was to him nothing more than "the rabblement." AE, whose Hermeticism he despised, was promoting whatever stock I had. Perhaps Joyce thought of me then as one of those whom he later described as:

> *Those souls have not the strength that mine has*
> *Steeled in the school of old Aquinas.*

But he seemed to be kin, at this stage, with his own "comedian Capuchin." The gestures he made with the ashplant he now carried, his way of making his voice raucous, were surely part of an act. And wasn't there, too, in his behavior the assertion of a young man conscious of his hand-me-down clothes, whose resort was the pawn office, who was familiar with the houses in Nighttown? The raucous voice, the ob-

scene limericks delivered with such punctilio . . . Was he
playing Rimbaud? Villon?

It appeared that Joyce had brought back from Paris a caba-
ret song, "Cadet Rousele," and would sing it at certain gather-
ings. So Oliver Gogarty had that name for him too: "Have
you seen Cadet Rousele?" The name suited the figure that,
yachting cap on his head, tennis shoes on his feet, ashplant
in hand, perambulated the streets of Dublin: Cadet Rousele.
It was as though there were two projections of Joyce in those
days, one his own person and the other the comic *persona*
with which Gogarty invested him.

I recall meeting the pair one Sunday morning on the South
Circular Road. It may have been that they were on their way
to see me, for I was living nearby. As they were north-side men
who seldom took a turn above Stephen's Green, they must
have had some object in coming this way on a Sunday morning. I was wearing a new suit, a fact that Gogarty immediately
dramatized: "Bardolph is dressed today!" The slender Joyce
with the steely blue eyes was still youthful enough—"jejune,"
as Buck Mulligan has it—to have fluffiness along his cheeks.
"Gone now!" Gogarty implied by a gesture as Joyce went on
a little ahead. "I got him to shave," he told me triumphantly.
"I showed him Dante's profile." Joyce never looked so Dan-
tesque afterward as he did in those days; later he wore glasses,
which not only took from the line of his face but covered what
seemed to be his penetrating gaze.

It was solely as a "character," and that partly a Gogartian
creation, that Joyce was known to Dubliners of that time. To
himself, of course, he was altogether different: he had none of
the approachableness, privately, of a "character":

> *That high, unconsortable one—*
> *His love is his companion.*

But since the early Ibsen article he had written nothing, beyond the Mangan essay and a few lyrics shown to friends, so
far as anyone knew. That he was an intellectually exceptional
young man anyone who met him could tell, but they also knew
he had frequently been in the gutter. There had been other
brilliant young Dubliners who were now but fading "charac-

ters." Needless to say, no one foresaw *Ulysses* or *Portrait of the Artist* or even *Dubliners*.

And so when it was known that he had begun a novel—it must have been the first version of *Portrait of the Artist*—his writing was regarded as a performance. "Have you heard about Joyce's Meredithean novel?" one of the coterie that included Joyce and Gogarty said to me. Of course, what Joyce was writing was not "Meredithean," but whatever it was, it would have to be something unexpected and improbable—hence the term —to be the product of this "character." My informant added an example of the writing: "the chocolate-colored train."

About that time an early play of mine was produced by the National Theatre Society. Joyce asked me to let him see the script. I did. Afterward I encountered him in O'Connell Street, and he treated me to a private "performance." Pointing his ashplant at me, he said, "I do not know from which of them you derive the most misunderstanding—Ibsen or Maeterlinck." He had the script with him: the encounter must have been planned. It was in a roll, which permitted him to make its presentation to me significant. "Rotten from the foundation up," he said.

Joyce and Gogarty were rarely seen then one without the other. Many years afterward, in Paris when he was nearing the end of *Finnegans Wake*, Joyce asked me to read Butler's *Hudibras* for him. (He was then virtually blind.) And what did he expect me to get for him out of the task he set me? Something about that companionship, dialectical in its relationship, that appears in a few great books—that of Don Quixote and Sancho Panza, Pantagruel and Panurge. It was an item in the comprehensiveness he wanted to attain. I read and reported back on *Hudibras*, but I never discovered any result. I wonder now if the duality which is also antithetical was not in the companionship between Oliver Gogarty and himself. Joyce, who to Gogarty was "Kinch the knifeblade," was constantly seeking for "the whetstone." Did the robust, well-dressed Gogarty, accustomed to taking the lead, know that he was the whetstone to the shabby, down-at-heel comedian of this period?

The two seemed to be engaged in some enterprise. An apostolate of irreverence! The rationalism of Catholicism and the nonrationalism of Protestantism, the nonsensicalness of Irish nationalism, the stupidity of British imperialism were satirized by them in verse and anecdote. What was creative was far from being let off. Joyce's ridicule of my play was to be expected, perhaps, but even Yeats was brought into mocking limericks. That the pair were collaborating on an anthology of inscriptions in public lavatories was known in their set and was regarded as a philosophers' *divertissement*.

Joyce and Gogarty had a follower, another medical student. The follower, John Elwood, admired Joyce without any understanding of his intellectual capacity but merely on account of his and Gogarty's wittiness and adventurousness. In relating their doings, less with gusto than incredulity, his expression seemed to say, "What will they think of next?" Himself he asserted along another line. He was a Republican according to the French revolutionary tradition, and in sending postal cards to people he knew he always addressed them as "Citizen" So-and-So. He became known as "Citizen" Elwood, or "the Citizen." Joyce conferred this designation, in *Ulysses*, on quite a different person—on the frieze-clad, bearded Michael Cusack, the founder of the Gaelic Athletic Association. Well, there was Joyce with his dream of reforming literature—perhaps even then of forging a conscience for his race—and there was Citizen Elwood with his Liberty, Equality, Fraternity, and they were about town together. Was Elwood a second whetstone?

## V. PADRAIC COLUM

"Lost angel of a ruined Paradise." It was James Cousins who, after he had stood Joyce and me to supper at the Vegetarian Restaurant, said this about my fellow guest. Our host—he was a little older than we were—asked Joyce urbanely what he was working on, and thereupon Joyce, parodying the "folk" style in current Irish writing, recited a curse he had put upon some Zoe or Kitty in Nighttown. The idealistic, tolerant North of Ireland poet, one of the early writers for the National Theatre Society that developed into the Abbey Theatre, was not amused.

Then, after the mock turkey, the gooseberry tart, and the cup of coffee had been consumed, the dinnerless convive went into another phase. Joyce spoke of the dedication of the artist with all the sincerity and eloquence he was to put into some of Stephen Dedalus' speeches. Outside, as we watched the slender, shabby figure with the ashplant go away from us, Cousins made his statement of regret and admiration for Joyce.

Neither Cousins nor I, because of our involvement in the nationalist movement, could at that time be a familiar of Joyce's. Still, I did about then see another side of him—not the "Kinch" of the Gogartian companionship nor the sensitive and dedicated writer, but the James Joyce of an intelligent fellowship. Gogarty and I had a mutual friend (I think it was Gogarty who brought us together), Tom Kettle. Kettle was regarded as the rising young man of the country. Like Joyce he had been through the Jesuit school at Clongowes Wood, and like Joyce was a University College man. I remember an afternoon he and I and Joyce and Gogarty spent together by the beach at Sandymount, near where Kettle lived at the time. Kettle's Catholicism was reinforced by the neo-Thomism (though it was not called that then), and Joyce's dialectics and Gogarty's jokes were competently and good-humoredly dealt with by him. I believed from the conversation that Joyce and Kettle were close friends; but speaking to Joyce afterward, I was surprised to learn he hardly knew Kettle and did not like him—he thought him too demonstrative.

On one thing, but with a difference in intention, Kettle and Joyce agreed: the necessity for getting Ireland back into Europe. Having lived in Paris, Joyce was not encouraging. "When you say you are *Irlandais* they think they have misunderstood you, that what you said was '*Hollandais*.'" Evidently for Joyce there was humiliation in the fact that his country had lagged so far behind that Europeans had no way of distinguishing Irish people. (But I found myself that the identification of "*Irlandais*" and "*Hollandais*" was due to the "r" not being rolled by the speaker.) Did Joyce really mean to insist on national identity?

He took some stock, it is true, in racialism—an abstract racialism, if one can use such a term. I never heard him discuss it, but at a point some years after this, when he was writing *Exiles*, he did identify himself with a generalized Celticism. His Celtia, however, had no history and no politics; its citizens were literally a chosen people (among the philosophers he claimed for it were Balfour and Bergson as well as Berkeley and Hume). Celtia, one supposes, stood out from what was for him the unattractive English-speaking civilization; it made on the spirit one claim only—to be distinguished.

And although for Joyce the post-Parnell Irish nationalism was only a noise in the street, a movement of the crowd of which he would never consider himself a part, he desired the independence of his country and he honored those who had striven disinterestedly for it. When the old Fenian leader, John O'Leary, died in 1907, Joyce paid tribute to him. For Parnell himself, from his earliest to his latest days, he felt hero worship. (Of course Joyce, like several other Irishmen of his and the generation before, identified himself with Parnell. Writing about the Irish situation years later in a Trieste paper, he said: "In his last proud appeal to the Irish People Parnell implored them not to throw him to the English wolves that were howling around him. It reflects honor on his countrymen that they did not fail his desperate appeal. They did not throw him to the English wolves; they tore him to pieces themselves."[1]) In Trieste, Joyce followed political developments in Ireland with intentness and comprehension. When Arthur Griffith promulgated a new policy, in 1906, Joyce was able to state the issue clearly: "Either Sinn Fein or Imperialism will conquer the present Ireland," he prophesied in a letter to his brother.[2]

Despite his seriousness in the conversation with Kettle, the Joyce all of us knew best at this period was the shabbily

[1] From *Il Piccolo della Sera*, May 16, 1912. Quoted in translation by Italo Svevo in his memoir, *James Joyce* (New York, 1950).

[2] Quoted in Herbert Gorman's *James Joyce* (New York, 1939), p. 186.

dressed, penniless, lewd-spoken youth whose disreputability was striking because of the witticisms that rose out of it. From all the fellows who related his sayings and doings he had been the borrower of small sums (he listed them all and acknowledged receipt, reportedly, by remarking on the disproportion in worth between the borrower and the lender).

One night he appeared with a companion—Oliver Gogarty, I think—at a rehearsal that was being conducted by members of the National Theatre Society. It was an intrusion, and the stage manager, W. G. Fay, was indignant. But Joyce appeared to be on his good behavior, and the girls of the cast went over to talk to him as a distinguished visitor. They had been recruited from a nationalist organization with a name that meant "The Daughters of Ireland." The two who entered into conversation with Joyce remembered him with great interest.

Now the hall where the rehearsal was being held was alongside and back of a provision shop in a middling street, and its entrance was by a passage between shops. Before this I had been told by his companion, "Joyce gets drunk in the legs, not the head. The other night I took him home and he was curled up in the cab like a tobacco spit." It must have been that he was drunk on this particular night, for Joyce became recumbent in the passage from the hall to the street, a matter which is recorded in *Ulysses*: "—O, the night in the Camden hall when the Daughters of Erin had to lift their skirts to step over you." Years afterward, in Paris, my wife and I took one of the aforesaid Daughters to see Joyce. She revealed that she was one who stepped over him in the dark passage. He shook his head mournfully. "I was too drunk to see your legs. What drink makes us miss!"

Another time Joyce was among those in the National Library when I was; readers were departing. Timing my exit to be with Joyce's, who was at the turnstile with a friend, ready to leave, I left some volumes on the counter. They were *The World as Will and Idea*. When the three of us were on the stairway, Joyce said with the raillery he often used when addressing me in those days, "You see before you two frightful examples of the will to live."

Which meant that Joyce and his companion were out to pick up girls. The companion was taciturn, but I guessed it

was he who knew the approaches. We went up Kildare Street
and along Harcourt Street to the road off which I lived, the
South Circular Road, which, with the lonesomeness of the
canal banks adjacent, was a likely place for pickups. As we
went along Joyce talked in a way that was supposed to be a
revelation to me of the uncloistered life. In those days he
would have relished playing Mephistopheles to Faust; later
he was extremely fastidious in his conversation.

His mind mustn't have been totally preoccupied with prospects on the South Circular Road, for after we had cups of
tea in a confectioner's in Harcourt Street and went strolling
again, we shifted to the World as Idea. Ibsen, remember, was
the avatar of the time. I spoke of having seen a nonprofessional
performance of *A Doll's House* and of George Moore's saying
to me at the end of it, "Sophocles! Shakespeare! What are
they to this!" Joyce's comment made the elder writer's seem
filled with boyish enthusiasm. "A postcard written by Ibsen
will be regarded as interesting and so will *A Doll's House*."
But when we talked of *Hedda Gabler* Joyce showed his admiration for the Master while allowing me to say all the enthusiastic things.

Then he repeated in the original Norwegian a lyric of Ibsen
about water lilies. His pronunciation of the words of the
poem could not have been, I now realize, any better than that
of a German with a few English lessons speaking a lyric of
Shakespeare in the original. But as Joyce repeated the lines
I had an image of floating flowers brought over into a verse
music that I longed to match. The poem that I could never
really know became for me a rhythmic challenge.

By this time we had reached the avenue that I lived on; I
left the pair, who as far as I could see were still without
prospects.

## VI.  PADRAIC COLUM

Never seeing Joyce in the homes of his family's friends must have given me a one-sided picture of him. The mannerly, spirited, whimsical Joyce of whom a glimpse is given in Eugene Sheehy's *May It Please the Court*[1] was outside my ken. That Joyce, who had gone places with his mother, "linking her towards the piano with grave Old World courtesy," belonged to a period that, socially and domestically, was over for him.

Sheehy portrays "Jim" with cane, hat, and eyeglass, swaggering up and down the room in the manner of a leading vaudeville singer of the day and singing with gusto, "The Man Who Broke the Bank at Monte Carlo." This young performer had a wide range of ballads, English and Irish, and loved to sing a certain half-comic, half-plaintive Irish love song. "I have heard him sing this ballad so often," says his contemporary and boyhood friend, who is now Judge Sheehy, "that I still remember every word of it." The song had two verses, of which the first ran:

> *Oh, Molly, I can't say you're honest,*
> *Sure you've stolen the heart from my breast.*
> *I feel like the bird that's astonished*
> *When the young vagabonds steal its nest.*
> *So I'll throw up a stone at the window,*
> *And in case any glass I should break,*
> *It's for you all the panes that I'm taking,*
> *Yerra! what wouldn't I smash for your sake.*

And the refrain was:

> *Ochone! Pillaloo! Och I'm kilt!*
> *May the quilt*
> *Lay light on your delicate form,*
> *When the weather is hot*

[1] Dublin, 1951.

*But my love, when 'tis not,*
*May it cradle you cosy and warm.*
*Nic nurum ni roo,*
*Nic norum ni!*

Judge Sheehy, who gives us this ballad and shows us this side of "Jim's" life, notes that many of the humorous items Joyce sang were from his father's repertoire: "The song commencing ' 'Tis youth and folly makes young men marry,' which Joyce heard his father singing in Victoria Hotel, Cork, as described in *Portrait,* was also a favourite of the son and I often heard him sing it. He sang these old favourite ballads of his father, too, with 'the quaint accent and phrasing' to which Joyce refers in the book."

Joyce's family life changed greatly with the death of his mother. I recall his saying to me, "Doors are being closed on me," which suggested that the social world in which he had moved was being narrowed. Did he want me to bring him into other houses? As far as I remember it he did, but I do not believe the houses I had access to would have provided entertainment for Joyce.

He was living with his father, brothers, and sisters, and the household was maintaining itself on credit, loans, and sales of anything that was still salable. Joyce earned a few pounds a month doing reviews for London and Dublin journals, but this left him on the ragged edge as far as food and clothes were concerned, and the shillings he contributed for the family's pressing daily needs must have left him literally penniless for days at a time.

But the son of John Stanislaus Joyce had grown up among such shifts. " 'His lordship!'—that's how we referred to the bailiff," he told me once. That he said it good-humoredly is worth noting. And with good humor he described on another occasion a familiar exploit in the Dublin of that day: the removal by hand or handcart of furniture from a dwelling where the rent collector could no longer be stood off to one that had (pro tem) a less exigent landlord. Joyce's own part in this particular removal was the carrying of two family portraits, one under each arm; I can imagine his humming an Italian air as the family deployed in the moonlight. The traditional way of carrying off such shifts was to turn them into japes or, if one had not the wit to do that, to be brassy or impudent about them. And here was James Joyce, essentially a gentleman, a man of learning, practicing the shifts with the traditional accompaniments.

He must have been actually hungry when, one afternoon, he came to where I worked and asked me to take him home to share my dinner. I was in lodgings at the time, and as Joyce and I went toward them I had misgivings about the meal we might be presented with. It was Lent, and my landlady was strict about having her boarders keep the fast. My worst fears were realized. The dish was fish and fish of the least flavorsome kind. The meal must indeed have been penitential, for I don't remember any sally of Joyce's at the table. He was downcast, probably reflecting on how miserable it was to depend for a meal on a man who had such small culinary resources. As a host I felt very let down or worse: an exhibit of scanted hospitality. But Joyce said nothing to reproach me.

No matter how hungry or how shabbily he was dressed, he always had fine composure. His face with the blue eyes was resolved. He would repeat a lyric or a limerick, relate a bawdy incident, or discuss a point in aesthetics in an unruffled, deliberate way. Not even a compliment to his writing could disturb him. Once, when I mentioned that I had read an article of his, he replied in a way that was characteristic of the matter and the manner of his speech: "I received for it thirty shillings which I immediately consecrated to Venus Pandemos."

One day Joyce came to me with a request for the loan of a half-sovereign. A financial scheme was involved in its use. He had been given a pawn ticket as a contribution to a fund he was raising for himself. Now, to anyone else a pawn ticket would be a minus quantity, but to Joyce it was realizable. The ticket was for books, and six shillings was the amount they were in for. As the ticket had been contributed by a medical student, Joyce told me, the books were undoubtedly medical, and so of value. And we would take them to our friend George Webb on the Quays, and sell them, and make fifty or even a hundred per cent on the transaction.

So we handed out the money with its interest, at Terence Kelly's pawn shop, and the books came across the counter to us. Hastily we undid the wrappings. And lo and behold! the books were an unsalable edition of the Waverley Novels of Sir Walter Scott, with one volume missing.

Sitting outside his shop, with his one closed and his one open eye, George Webb received Joyce cordially. "Some of your Italian books, Mr. Joyce?" Joyce had taken Italian at University College, spoke it elegantly and fluently, and had picked up a lot of valuable Italian books which he was selling at the time. "No, Webb; these are special," replied Joyce. We opened the parcel and exhibited the wretched set of romances. Very loftily indeed did Joyce talk to the most knowing book-seller in Dublin. "But you have brought some Italian books with you, haven't you, Mr. Joyce?"

When Webb gathered that Joyce really wanted to sell him the books in the parcel and that he had ransomed them from Terence Kelly's on the prospect of selling them, he had them wrapped up again for us. This most estimable of bookbuyers and booksellers, this George Webb of the swivel eye, was generally found seated meditatively outside his shelves and stacks; he mentioned quietly and firmly the price he would give or take. Across from him on the Quay was the shop of the black-bearded Hickey, who looked like a buccaneer rather than a bookseller, and who would come roaring out of the reaches of his shop and beat you down if you wanted to sell, or would shamelessly boost the prices marked on the books on the stands outside if you wanted to buy. But George Webb was sympathetic to the book-wanter and the book-disposer. His fairness was recognized. If by chance and unknowingly you brought him the most sought-for book or pamphlet, say, Shelley's *Address to the Irish People*, the price he offered you would be the proper price. Now he said mildly to us, "Take the books back to Terence Kelly's; maybe you can get him to let you have back the six shillings." We took them back and did manage to get our six shillings.

The Dubliners of *Ulysses*—the Dubliners of James Joyce's young manhood—are a very strange tribe; they all seem to be small-scale promoters with ideas for making money and improving their financial, intellectual, and physical conditions, ideas that will never be realized. They are always ready to talk and to give an account of themselves and their neighbors. They are a people of phenomenal leisure, up to many shifts; they are constantly engaged in thinking out ways and means of getting "passes"—passes to theaters or passes on the railway. They have a fund of cant phrases that fit every occasion. And there isn't a businessman among them.

Joyce himself concocted schemes for making money that Leopold Bloom, but with much less precision, might have sponsored. One day he came to me, not to borrow money, but not at all casually either: he came with a definite objective. He had a scheme that he was really sold on. Why he came to consult me about it will always be an impenetrable mystery.

His project was nothing less than the establishment of a daily newspaper in Dublin. As I listened with incredulity he elaborated. He told me about the format it would have, the sort of articles that would appear in it. It would be along the lines of a Continental newspaper, published in the afternoon, and its establishment would cost . . . I have forgotten the figure, though Joyce, I recall, was exact about the amount that was needed. It was in any case a sum that in Dublin of that day was fabulous. And this penniless and jobless young man was out to raise that much capital. He had even taken the trouble to have the name of the paper registered: it was to be called *The Goblin*.

What he wanted me to do was to help him make contacts —I, who was as far removed from moneyed people as he himself was—with people with whom he could discuss organization and finance. He asked me especially did I know any Jewish people he could go to with the project. (It is odd that the creator of the most outstanding Jew in modern literature did not at that time know any of the Jewish community in Dublin.) Jews would be receptive to such a proposition, Joyce thought. I had two Jewish friends, intellectuals, Willy and Harry Sinclair, who had an antique shop in Nassau Street. I brought Joyce into the shop and introduced him to one or the other of the brothers. Of course nothing came of it in the way of promoting *The Goblin*, and I don't know whether my introduction resulted in any friendliness between the parties. However, one of the Sinclairs gets a line in *Ulysses*:

Bloom at one stage along his itinerary remarks, "Have a chat
with young Sinclair? Well-mannered fellow."

While Joyce was still pursuing the *Goblin* idea, I mentioned to him that I had a friend, an American of Irish de-
scent, who was well enough off to occupy a great house in
County Kildare. Joyce actually made his way to this house,
going and coming on foot and returning in the middle of the
night, after my friend had refused to see this unannounced
stranger. Joyce then wrote the man an indignant letter. Years
afterward, in our apartment in Paris, the two, who had never
seen each other, came together. I took each aside and told
him who the other was, reminding them of their near-
encounter. Each was astonished; Joyce was amused at the
recollection of the unfulfilled mission.

The Dublin in which Joyce pursued such schemes, the city
that came to be recorded in *Portrait of the Artist* and with so
much more abundance in *Ulysses*, belongs to a closed epoch.
Dublin is no longer a small city, contained within boundaries
in which everybody encounters everybody else; throngs of its
people now live outside the old Dublin, in bus-reached places
the names of which used to evoke distance and the sense of
pastoral charm—the Donneycarneys of Stephen Dedalus and
his contemporaries. The early Dublin was pre-motorbus, pre-
cinema. Its old men and young men, its women and girls
abounded in talk of operas and musical plays; they could recite
fragments of public speeches. The city was oral as no other in
Western Europe was. The Dublin of today does not sing, does
not quote from poems and orations; the days of the Carl Rosa
Opera are remote; the Gaiety Theatre is no longer attended
by enthusiastic playgoers—Dublin is cinema-minded now. The
*Freeman's Journal*, that dignified representative of the national newspaper tradition, and the *Evening Telegraph*, a
four-page supplement to the day's news in which even the
advertisements were garrulous, have passed away; their offices, which used to be haunts of news-providers and news-
seekers, are closed, and their editors, leader-writers, and re-
porters, who were well-known Dublin characters (the editor
of the *Evening Telegraph*, who appears in *Ulysses* as Myles
Crawford, was, with his shock of white hair, his rubicund face,

his tumultuous reaction to everything, intended from all time to be an epical character) are all gone. Only those who knew the Dublin of that closed epoch can catch the full flavor of *Ulysses*, particularly its comic overtones.

But the old Dublin had its bad side too: impoverishment, for Joyce, and with it the absence of a milieu in which a young man of talent could circulate. The houses that Joyce passed in the evening, on his way to a pub in the hope that some fellow there would stand him a drink or on his way to a supperless home, those grand houses with their drawing rooms, the spacious gardens before them, the maids to polish their door brasses in the morning, knew nothing of the existence of any such young man of intellectual distinction. Some Trinity College student who had passed his examination for the Indian Civil Service—such, to the inhabitants of those houses, was the embodiment of "intellectual distinction." That a prospectless young man walking by their terrace of houses and gardens was thinking of forging a conscience for them would have been regarded as the quaintest of quaint conceits.

## VII.   PADRAIC COLUM

Everyone who has read *Ulysses* has some impression of the Martello tower on the beach, with its outlook over Dublin Bay, that Joyce occupied about this period. The author of *Finnegans Wake*, knowing that this tower and some score of others had been built as defenses against an expected Napoleonic invasion, would have found much significance in the structure, regarding it as a memento of a struggle between opposites—historically between Napoleon and Wellington. The fact that the opposites had something identical in them —that the towers intended for use against the Corsican were of Corsican origin, as I have lately learned—would have been of even greater significance to the later Joyce. An article in a 1955 issue of *The Blarney Magazine* says that "During an

English attack on the French garrison at Mortella Point in Corsica, this small tower held out for days against heavy bombardment from English naval vessels. The English were so impressed that they built them all along the south and east coasts of England and Ireland." And that the Martello towers were never used for the purpose for which they were built would also have had meaning for the later Joyce, to whom the blurred edges were as much a part of history as the clear text.

I am familiar with the particular tower that Joyce lived in. However, I take its measurements from the description given in *The Blarney Magazine*:

*They are of very sturdy construction, with solid stone walls eight feet thick, having a staircase built in the thickness of the walls. They are comprised of two floors with a gun platform on top for two or three guns, and also a place for pouring molten lead or burning oil down on the unfortunate enemy who approached it. In a covered recess on the roof is a place for heating cannon balls. . . . The towers could only be entered by mounting an iron ladder leading to a door twenty feet above the ground. The door could only be opened by a copper key which would not give off sparks.*

The copper key guaranteed not to emit sparks that would set off powder kegs fascinates me. A time came when the keys changed from sergeants' to sojourners' hands. About 1900 the British War Office in Ireland decided definitely that Martello towers were obsolete as defense structures and, removing the guns from their tops and withdrawing the little garrisons from beside them, offered them for rental—unfurnished, of course. The tenants attracted were parties of young men, continuous occupants though their personnel changed frequently, who wanted to swin, bathe, loaf on the beaches. For such the tower on the north and the tower on the south side of Dublin were ideal. The rent, I think, was a pound a month. A few cots, chairs, shelves, cooking utensils were all that was needed for what was really just an encampment. There was a fireplace.

The tower on the south side was in Sandycove, six or seven miles out of the city, twenty minutes by train or electric tram. Here, in 1904, James Joyce, with Oliver Gogarty and another young man who appears in *Ulysses* under the name of Haines, took up residence. I was never in the tower during their occupancy, but a year later, when Oliver Gogarty, the poet Seumas O'Sullivan, and Arthur Griffith, the founder of Sinn Fein and the editor of its journal, made it their quarters, I spent a few week ends there.

Mounting the outside ladder and entering through a narrow door, one found oneself in a spacious circular room, dark because it was lighted only through window slits. Going up the stairway in the wall one came out into clear daylight. A sentry wall went around the top of the tower, on which were gun rests that could be used for writing purposes. One looked toward the harbor of Dunleary, the city, the promontory of Howth, and, turning 'round, toward the charming eminence of Killiney. Below on the beach were bathing places—a discreet strip for ladies, to the left, and the men's bathing place right below. The pool was named the Forty Foot Hole; only practiced swimmers were supposed to use it. The rest of the beach was rocky.

It was an exciting place to be in. Poets could be expectant of inspiration there. Indeed Oliver Gogarty anticipated the production of a classic:

> *All ye who dig for treasure trove*
> *Beneath the tower of Sandycove,*
> *What joy if you could only seize*
> *One Sapphic fragment, or unroll*
> *A tender twilight-litten scroll*
> *Of Starkey's hazel trees!*

"Starkey" is Seumas O'Sullivan, whose best known lyric at the time was the evocative "It is a whisper among the hazel bushes." Gogarty's inscription has been justified—it is "out," as one says of a dream. For there are pilgrimages now to the tower of Sandycove, though not for the sake of any verse written there. It is famous today as the setting of the somber comedy in which Stephen Dedalus, Buck Mulligan, Haines, and the old milk vendor had parts.

From one who knew the scene and the personages a comment on that comedy is in order. Joyce's treatment of the young man whom he calls Haines is questionable. He wants to confront the incarnation of the traditional Ireland, the Poor Old Woman who appears as the milk vendor, with three characters—one who has renounced allegiance to her, one who is her conqueror, one who is her gay betrayer. He gave Haines the role of the conqueror. But surely the conqueror should manifest the traits of the soldier and the administrator. Haines shows no such traits: he is the student all through the scene. Far from imposing anything on her, he is asking for the Poor Old Woman's good will.

Joyce found himself living in the tower in 1904 with a young man who was Gogarty's guest, a young man who spoke with an Oxford accent, who had done what young Englishmen could afford to do—traveled in out-of-the-way places— and who probably mentioned that members of his family were in the British army or the British diplomatic service. Needing an Englishman in the scene, Joyce cast this young man for the part. So insistent is he on the alien presence of Haines that he throws in the seventeenth-century proverb about the three things to beware of—"horn of a bull, hoof of a horse, smile of a Saxon." And yet so sure is the drawing that one recognizes in Haines a young man who was very well known in various Dublin circles at the time—and known mainly for his pro-Irish activities.

His name was Trench. He belonged to a family whose most distinguished member was Richard Chevenix Trench, Archbishop of Dublin, who wrote a book long well known in classrooms—On the Study of Words. That family might at one time have called themselves Anglo-Irish, for they belonged to the Protestant minority in Ireland, were landowners, opposed the nationalist movement, entered the British services. The hyphenated appellation was discarded by the younger generation. They were Irish Irelanders. Samuel Chevenix Trench was a name that required a good deal of ingenuity to Gaelicize. The bearer of it just dropped the "Samuel Chevenix" and substituted the romantic Gaelic "Dermott" (or, in another spelling, Diarmuid). He was known as Dermott Trench at the time of his residence in the tower at Sandycove.

After leaving Oxford and making a world tour, Trench had come back to Ireland to take a place in a movement that looked like a national resurgence, that had enlisted all that was patriotic in a minority that opposed the "Ireland a nation" idea. For a young man in Dublin, Trench was in an enviable position: he had an independent income; he could go here and there and do this and that. One of the things he did was to make himself a fluent speaker of Irish. He belonged to various organizations that worked to promote cultural and economic interests; he assisted AE in the editing of *The Irish Homestead*; he belonged to a theater group that put on plays in Irish.

The latter group, to which I also belonged, wanted to put on a play in Irish—Douglas Hyde's *Casadh an t-Sugain*. The chief part is that of an arrogant vagabond poet who, coming into a house on the eve of a wedding, so fascinates the prospective bride that she takes no account of anyone else. He has to be got rid of. But as there is something sacred about a poet he cannot be manhandled; he is got out of the door by a trick and then refused re-entry. Dermott Trench was picked for the part. I remember having seen three or four actors play this role, but I do not recall any one of them's having impressed me so much as he did. Exuberance is the characteristic of Hanrahan, the poet, and Dermott Trench went the limit in exuberance. By a stroke of genius he garbed himself in a cast-off hunting jacket of scarlet, thus making us visualize the vagabondage of the poet, dependent on hand-me-downs, and the arrogance that claimed a cavalier's accouterment.

Trench, this sympathetic and cultivated, this engaging young man, ended his life by suicide. Looking back, I can see that he was what is now called a manic-depressive. I never saw him in his depressive state. As I knew him and as my friends of the time knew him, he was helpful, disinterested, visionary. I hope there is a record of him somewhere, beyond the anecdote I have set down here, to distinguish him from the Haines of *Ulysses*.

One can hardly write about the inhabitants of the tower and leave Oliver St. John Gogarty undelineated. But there is Buck Mulligan, the most living portrait in literature: he appears, he moves, he talks. Why put a sketch alongside that full-length portrait?

Nevertheless, for the sake of conformity with other descriptions of Joyce's familiars, Buck Mulligan has to appear—and nowhere in this book more fittingly than here—as this writer knew him. His home was in one of the fine squares that belong to Dublin's eighteenth century—Rutland Square. Gogarty's family, consisting by the time I knew him of a widowed mother and another son, also had a spacious house outside the city, in Clontarf. His father, a brilliant medical man, had died fairly young. Apparently Dr. Gogarty senior had had to work his way up in order to enter the profession: Simon Dedalus, always ready to denigrate persons of any pretensions, speaks of the one with whom his son is associating as "A counterjumper's son. Selling tapes in my cousin, Peter-Paul McSwiney's"—which means that for a time the medical aspirant had had a job in a department store. The elder Gogarty's wife had a considerable fortune: she was a Miss Oliver of Galway. Like all Galway people she was very "conscious"; she was inclined to look down on people who did not live in one of the squares of Dublin that still had a suggestion of aristocracy.

Doctors formed an elite in the Dublin of that time, in which social life was professional, bureaucratic, mercantile. Sir William Wilde, the father of Oscar Wilde, was, in a previous generation, the representative of that able, learned, versatile group. It produced marked characters; it produced men with unusual social gifts. That Oliver Gogarty should have chosen to follow his father's profession was not surprising.

Although his family was Catholic, Gogarty did not go through the usual Jesuit school; he went—and this was perhaps a mark of snobbery—through a Catholic school in England. He did not go to the university that most young men of Catholic families in Dublin went to either; he took his courses in the Anglican Dublin University (Trinity College). Trinity had men of great erudition at the time: Dowden in English, Tyrrell in Latin, and, most notable of all, Mahaffy, the man who had instructed Oscar Wilde—famous for his wit, conversation, snobbery, and also for his outstanding Greek scholarship. And so the medical student who appears in *Ulysses* as Buck Mulligan had exceptional tutors, and he himself was no backward student.

He had a defect that prevented his being a companionable man—the gravest of defects, perhaps: he had no reserve in speaking about people, even those whom he had cause to admire, even those who were close to him. If they had some pitiful disability or shortcoming, he brought it right out. It was an incontinence of speech with Gogarty that was in itself a defect. One might think it was for the sake of making a witty point that he maligned others, and sometimes it was that. But, exposed to it for a while, one began to see that the trait was basic: Oliver Gogarty could not help but see some oddness, infirmity, or delinquency in a person talked about. The result was that people gave him license and kept a distance from him.

But as I write this there comes before me the solid figure of the founder of Sinn Fein, Arthur Griffith. In times subsequent to those I am writing about, Griffith and Gogarty became friends. Griffith trusted him. That means that Gogarty had a side that a political leader could respect. Other historically important people were familiar with him too. I shall only refer to the impression that, in later years, Gogarty made on Yeats. Yeats at the time was obsessed with the idea of the man of action who was also the man of meditation. (I heard him say to my surprise that Oscar Wilde could have been a great man of action—someone like Disraeli.) And Yeats was greatly impressed with Oliver Gogarty—an airman and a surgeon, a wit and a poet.

There are other things to be said in Gogarty's favor. I remember an instance of his impulsive generosity. At the time of his friendship with Joyce I was working in a railway office in Kildare Street. As I was paid monthly, I could around payday lend a student friend a half-crown or even a half-sovereign, as I sometimes lent Joyce. One day, wearing a resplendent waistcoat, Gogarty came to the office and asked me for the loan of a half-sovereign. I told him I was just then in need of a half-sovereign myself. "Is that so?" Gogarty exclaimed, leaping away down the steps. In twenty minutes he was back, his coat buttoned up. He pressed a goldpiece into my hand. He had pawned the waistcoat and brought me the amount of the pledge.

Like many Dubliners of the time, Gogarty had a memory

stocked with poetry. In his case Greek and Latin were included in the mental volume: he could turn from Shelley to
Catullus, from Shakespeare to a chorus from Aeschylus or a
strophe of Pindar. He could repeat long passages from Burns
and other Scottish poets (he admired the Scotch bards immensely and rejoiced in their bawdiness) in what sounded
like braid Scots. He had an extraordinary readiness in striking
speech, and though there was an inconsequence in his mind,
it was an inconsequence that could make his sayings out-
rageously funny. I once brought him an invitation to a garden
party at which there would be male members of the Hermetic
Society. "Would my mother be raped by a mystic?" he said, as
if he were concentrating on some precaution.

He was not a good conversationalist. For one thing, there
was no continuity in his mind; nor was there much give-and-
take. He talked for effect—Gogartian effect. But a Gogartian
monologue, with its sudden shifts and inexplicable transitions,
its copious quotations of poetry along with frequent plain
statements of practical issues, was, in his young manhood
anyway, an astonishing verbal display. His genius was in his
power of uniting the comic and the poetic, as in "Leda and
the Swan."

Gogarty knew that his diversity of activities covered an
idleness. His defense, which is also a challenge, is in his epi-
gram on Petronius:

> *Proconsul of Bithynia,*
> *Who loved to turn the night to day,*
> *Yet for your ease had more to show*
> *Than others for their push and go.*
> *Teach us to save the Spirit's expense,*
> *And win to Fame through indolence.*

Joyce saw him in the tower as a Renaissance prelate. Gogarty
saw himself as a Roman, a man of the camp and the senate,
speaking a language of order and of command.

# VIII.  PADRAIC COLUM

It was in the summer of 1904 that I heard talk about a lute. Joyce was about to embark on a venture, it was said, in which he would play on a lute and sing to its accompaniment. Whether he had got an engagement for such a performance or whether it was a private venture was not disclosed. The venue of the lute-playing and singing was to be one of the English summer resorts, Brighton or Bournemouth.

I could easily see a slender figure in white trousers, canvas shoes, straw hat, and black jacket, a lute in his hands, promenading by the sea. The minstrel had not yet been displaced by the radio singer. There were music-hall performers who delighted crowds by their singing. Of course, their turns were comic, but Joyce did not look down on them for that. He could give a very good impersonation of the one who sang,

*At Trinity Church I met my doom.*

But in my imagination Joyce's line would be to restore to the English public the songs that the lute inspired:

*My lute, awake! perform the last*
*Labor that thou and I shall waste.*

Whoever first told me about this adventure of Joyce's regarded it as a sort of vagrancy, but the vagrancy of a fellow accomplished enough not to become more broke through it. When Joyce himself told me about the project—his follower, Citizen Elwood, was with him—he was earnest, as he had been the time he spoke to me of the *Goblin* enterprise. But standing with the companion, who expected witticisms from him, he could not help being a little mocking. "Personally conducted," he said, "like the Emperor Nero's tour in Greece." I never heard whether he made the tour or not, or if he did what the results were.

The lute-playing venture seems playful indeed by contrast

with the project I heard, later that summer or fall, Joyce was about to embark on. He was leaving Dublin to take up a job in a Berlitz School on the Continent, and he was not going alone: he was taking with him a Galway girl, Nora Barnacle, who had been working, it was said, in one of the better hotels in Dublin.

The financing of such a journey, as some of us could see, would be a troublesome and humiliating business for Joyce. Even in those days of cheap travel and cheap meals it would have taken twenty or thirty pounds, and for a young man doing casual teaching and casual writing twenty or thirty pounds was hard to come by. All the shabby difficulties of the impecunious lay between the decision to go and his and Nora Barnacle's departure.

"I'm not like Jesus Christ—I can't walk on the water," he said to me the last time I saw him in the National Library. I won't go so far as to say that there was something desperate about him on this occasion, but he was putting on the air of a desperado. Raising funds for the journey forced him into a sort of mendicancy. He spoke to me of approaching Lady Gregory. I expect he did, but if she helped him she did it very privately: there is no mention of a gratuity to Joyce in her published correspondence.

Joyce's one play reflects aspects of his and Nora's departure. The play is properly named. "It is not about an adultery," Joyce said to me in later years. "It is about exile." Their departure was not an emigration: it was a self-imposed exile. And James Joyce and Nora Barnacle were committing themselves to each other in a way that, because of its irregularity, was particularly tense—tragic even. But at that time, as they were leaving, the exile seemed temporary. There is no doubt that Joyce looked forward to a return to Ireland with Nora when he would be recognized and honored.

Joyce and Nora went from Dublin to Zurich, but it turned out there was no job for Joyce in the Swiss city. The couple had to hang around there, their funds dwindling, and then make another journey—this time to Trieste. Trieste proved another disappointment, and they had to move again, this time to Pola.

It was from Pola that Joyce sent back his parting shot at
Dublin and Dubliners, in the form of the broadside, "The
Holy Office," which he had printed in the Austrian city and
distributed to all those mentioned in it, late in 1904.

The piece is a satire on the Dublin intelligentsia, but it has
in it all the violence of Joyce's feelings toward the city as a
whole. Now the literature of insult is hard to achieve. There
should be rancor in it, but that rancor should be garbed in
insouciance:

> *When I saw the keeper frown,*
> *Tipping him with half-a-crown,*
> *Now, said I, we are alone,*
> *Name your heroes one by one.*
> *Who is that hell-featured brawler?*
> *Is it Satan? No, 'tis Waller.*
> *In what figure can a bard dress*
> *Jack, the grandson of Sir Hardress?*
> *Honest keeper, drive him further,*
> *In his looks are hell and murther;*
> *See the scowling visage drop*
> *Just as when he murdered Throp.*

This is Swift (a veteran writer, of course, whereas Joyce was
only twenty-two) on Dublin notables of his day, on the members of Parliament. The Joyce who wrote "The Holy Office"
has only rancor:

> *But all these men of whom I speak*
> *Make me the sewer of their clique.*
> *That they may dream their dreamy dreams*
> *I carry off their filthy streams*
> *For I can do those things for them*
> *Through which I lost my diadem,*
> *Those things for which Grandmother Church*
> *Left me severely in the lurch.*
> *. . . . . . . . . . . . . . .*
> *And though they spurn me from their door*
> *My soul shall spurn them evermore*

Here he is projecting a figure of himself that an unseasoned
young man would project. And there is the mock prayer that

he sent to his brother about the same time (quoted in Gorman's biography):

*. . . then, by the crucified Jaysus, if I don't sharpen that little pen and dip it into fermented ink and write tiny little sentences about the people who betrayed me, send me to hell. After all, there are many ways of betraying people. It wasn't only the Galilean suffered that.*

But who was James Joyce that he should have seventy disciples to send "against religion and government"? And who, in Heaven's name, betrayed him?


## IX. PADRAIC COLUM


Five years after he left Dublin I met the returned James Joyce in O'Connell Street. With him was a little boy, his four-year-old son Giorgio. In appearance, bearing, manner, Joyce was improved. If I say he was more assured I may be misunderstood, for in one sense Joyce was always assured. But there is a difference between the assurance of a man who has only intellectual capital and the assurance of a man who, besides that, has some sort of position. The Joyce I encountered in the street in 1909 had the assurance of position. He was no longer the "character," the "card," the "artist" of Dublin conversation.

Alluding to the fact that Giorgio spoke Italian, Joyce declared his satisfaction in his children being brought up in a Latin civilization. They would grow up with music too. Giorgio was already singing airs from operas. Since 1905 Joyce and Nora had been living in Trieste, where Giorgio and a second child, a daughter, had been born and where Joyce's brother Stanislaus had joined them. They had moved to Rome without Stanislaus for part of a year, but had not liked it there and had gone back to Trieste, where Joyce made a small but regular living by teaching first at the Berlitz School and later by giving private lessons in English. Trieste at the time

was Austrian, and Joyce liked the casualness—the "ram-
shackle" quality—of the Austrian Empire; Trieste became a
home city.

My concern here is not with the reported circumstances of
Joyce's life abroad, however, but only with the personal con-
tact I had with him. On this first of his visits back to Dublin,
I found him as I had known him or, if altered, a recognizable
Joyce.

One incident of this particular visit Joyce recalled affec-
tionately, relating it to me years afterward. I remember it as
illustrating the strong bond that was between him and his
father, a bond of which one strand was music. The incident
took place on an excursion made one afternoon by James
Augustine Joyce and John Stanislaus Joyce—Stephen Dedalus
and Simon Dedalus.

I never met the elder Joyce, though I had heard many
stories about him, and as my evaluation of the incident de-
pends on some impression of him, I have to characterize him
from sources outside my own. Decades after this a Dublin
journalist interviewed John Stanislaus (at his by-then-famous
son's request) and took down his discourse in shorthand, so
we have him in a long soliloquy.[1]

"I often told Jim to go for the Bar, for he has a great flow
of language and he speaks better than he writes. However, he
has done very well," was one of the things his father said in
that interview about the author of *Ulysses*. John Stanislaus
talks about his youth and early manhood without any sense
that anyone might consider it misspent. What books does he
mention? Divil a book! He has read only newspapers and
racing calendars. But he knows about music. He reminisces
about concerts and noted singers, about McGuckin, the tenor
of the Carl Rosa Company (who said that he, John Stanislaus,
had "the best tenor voice in Ireland"), and others. His
interests are hunting, racing, politics as a branch of sport,
"jollifications." Joyce portrayed his father as neglecting his
family with absolute nonchalance, using whatever money
came his way in entertaining cronies in bars and at race tracks.
He was a man who always had time to attend funerals of

[1] Given in *A James Joyce Year Book*, edited by Maria Jolas (Paris,
1949).

people he knew or even had only heard of. A ubiquitous, gregarious man!

And so, after five years apart, John Stanislaus Joyce and the son whom he was proud of mainly because he could hold his own on a platform, went into the country one afternoon, first taking a tram to the outlying village of Rathfarnham and then walking on. As they went along the quiet country road, the gossip of bars and committee rooms must have been poured into the ear of the author of *Dubliners* and the future begetter of *Ulysses*.

A spacious saloon called The Yellow House, some way out into the country, was their terminus. In a big room, empty at the time, there were two pianos. Refreshment having been ordered, the older man sat at one. He played a theme that asked, "Why did you go from us?" His son "Jim," at the other piano, played something in reply (he told me what it was, but I cannot remember). It was an epiphany of a sort, a showing forth of a relationship which was nearly always covered over, and Joyce dwelt on it later with some tenderness. There must have been something in his father that is not revealed in the speech of the Dublin "character" so bent on "jollifications." John Stanislaus Joyce did not impose himself, as Irish fathers thought it was their bounden duty to do, on his son. There was a relationship, and it was not shown overtly, but, as on this occasion, in a very sensitive fashion.

Perhaps it was the day after his excursion with his father that I met James Joyce by appointment in Bewley's Coffee Shop in Westmoreland Street. Bewley's was the afternoon resort of the intelligentsia at that period; it was delightful for its mocha coffee, its freshly baked cakes with fresh butter. Joyce was there ahead of me: I came in with several books under my arm.

At a meeting of this kind Joyce was wont to remain aloof, leaving it to the other person to open up. The books I was carrying were collections of the work of Samuel Ferguson, a poet who had influenced the young Yeats. His centenary was on and I was writing about him for the *Freeman's Journal*. I made an enthusiastic comment about one or two of the poems. Joyce picked up a volume, looked at the poem I mentioned, laid the book down, and like one resigned to his own disability said, "I couldn't read this."

We talked casually for a while. Then he said, "You had a poem in a magazine. Would you say it for me?" There was only one poem I had published for some time—"Across the Door," it is called. While I spoke the poem he listened with a sort of quiescence. Then he said, "I couldn't have written that." It was his only comment.

This was a friendly Joyce, a more mellow Joyce. And also a cavalier. For he showed me parchment pages with his poems copied out on them in his own hand. He was going to present them to Nora on one of their anniversaries; he had brought them to Dublin to have them bound in a certain style by a binder on the Quays whom he trusted. I went with him to the bindery. He told me of the design he was going to have stamped on the cover. According to my recollection there were to be two interlinking rings, with the mottoes of his family and hers around them. But I may be wrong in thinking this about the mottoes, for a letter from Nora Joyce to my wife and myself, after Joyce's death, describes the cover as having a different device.[2]


# X. PADRAIC COLUM


Joyce reappeared in Dublin later in 1909, to give the city its first moving-picture theater. I had heard that there was an invention called the cinematograph, which produced continuously moving pictures, but its public functioning was unknown to me. Joyce was the first to explain it all to me, when, hearing he was again in Dublin, I arranged to meet him somewhere.

Cinematograph theaters had now become a regular thing in Italy; there were several in Trieste, and the audience for them—if one might call it an audience—was growing. Joyce had been sent over to Ireland to establish a cinematograph

2 See p. 154.

theater in Dublin; Belfast and Cork were also to be given moving-picture houses through Joyce's pioneering. He had brought Italian workmen over with him, and the very day I saw him they were engaged in remodeling premises on Mary Street for the theater, to be called the Volta. The businessman Joyce of *The Goblin* reappeared in the Joyce of the Volta project, and I was impressed by the sort of authority he showed.

I was still more impressed when I stood with him inside the building that was being remodeled, and heard him give orders in Italian to the men at work. But I was troubled about one thing. Was this the site for a novel enterprise? Mary Street was on the verge of a slum area. Would people from the residential districts of Dublin come here? I had doubts. I supposed this was the only site available.

Joyce's first regularly published book, *Chamber Music*, had been brought out some time before that by a London firm. I had a copy of it, and at one of my meetings with him on this return trip in 1909, I talked to him about poems of his that were in my memory. "I am not a poet," he told me. This meant that he felt he was able to put more of himself into prose. (It meant, too, apparently, that he thought the published poems were too youthful, now, in terms of the prose he was writing. He had wanted, I later learned, to send a telegram to the publisher of *Chamber Music* to hold up publication, because he wished to appear first as a prose writer.)

It is true that the poems in *Chamber Music* seem to come out of a young musician's rather than a young poet's world. In the first of the sequence Love is a musician "with head to the music bent"; in the second "she bends upon the yellow keys"; in the third one awakens "to hear the sweet harps play / To Love before him on his way"; in the fourth there is "one who is singing by your gate"; in the fifth she is "singing and singing a merry air." The poet hears "the noise of waters"; he hears "an army charging upon the land, / And the thunder of horses plunging": a lady leans "to the shell of night" and harkens to sounds. *Chamber Music* has all that a musician looks for in a poet's arrangement of words—syllables that can be articulated, range of expression within little compass, situation, and, above all, the charm that is in the spontaneous rendering of a mood—when choosing verse to be set to music.

The young poet had definite musical interests at the time he was making these poems; he had made a setting himself for Mangan's "Veil not thy mirror, sweet Amine," and for several of Yeats' lyrics. Joyce's comrade of the early Dublin days, J. F. Byrne, speaks of Joyce's composing an accompaniment for Mangan's "Dark Rosaleen"; and one of the most fascinating glimpses we have of the Joyce of that time is in Byrne's account of how the pair used to go at night into a small room in which there was a pianoforte, a room off the Aula Maxima in University College. Byrne would listen to Joyce sing the airs he had in mind and then play them for him. "And sometimes on these nights, in order not to attract attention, we stayed in that room in pitch darkness—Joyce singing almost *sotto voce* and I playing the piano *pianissimo*."[1]

Joyce used to play and sing English songs, Elizabethan and Jacobean. "They are ample," he would say, contrasting their full-blooded gaiety with the mournfulness of Irish melodies. It may be because he was so completely possessed by this musical tradition that the poems he wrote are without a trace of Irish influence—except, perhaps, for the poem that is last in the collection. And yet I feel that I am not altogether exact in saying there is no Irish influence in these poems. They could not have been written in any other place than that city which so belatedly receives, so lingeringly lets go of, a tradition— Dublin, in which there was such little pressure of present intellectual interests that a student could project himself into another period.

Measured by its sales—probably fewer than fifty copies were sold there—*Chamber Music* had made very little impact on Dublin. Yet there were those among Joyce's townspeople who knew that this was not a slight performance. There were Dubliners who memorized some of the poems and repeated them on occasion. *Chamber Music* brought close to them the old squares with their high houses, the twilit roads that led out of the town along which sweethearts walked, the sound of the piano in old-fashioned drawing rooms. Some knew that these

[1] In Byrne's *The Silent Years* (New York, 1953).

were not merely recreations of Elizabethan and Jacobean song: there is drama in the sequence—youthful love, betrayal in friendship, exile. After A *Portrait of the Artist as a Young Man* came out, those who had *Chamber Music* in their minds could see that the novel repeated the drama of the lyric sequence.

To Yeats, *Chamber Music* was "a little of it very beautiful and all of it very perfect technically." He spoke of the last poem, "I hear an army charging upon the land," which appeared in an anthology as a "most lovely poem," and he mentions it again as "a technical and emotional masterpiece."[2] Thus the self-exiled Joyce was beginning to seem a potent figure to some of his countrymen.

But it was, as he himself said, as a prose writer that Joyce was to find himself. The "Meredithean" novel of the far-back days was being recast. His stories—two of which had appeared in *The Irish Homestead* and had seemed applications of the Flaubertian method to rather slight incidents of Dublin life—had been in the hands of Grant Richards of London. The English printers had objected to various passages in the manuscript and Richards had finally returned it. Then, on the invitation of one of the firm, the stories, *Dubliners*, had been submitted to the Dublin publishers, Maunsel and Company. After deliberating more than a year, Maunsels had given Joyce a contract earlier in 1909, and now, on this second visit to Dublin, he had been promised he would soon see proofs of his book.

This was all very good. Joyce's first serious book was going to be published in his native city, and meanwhile he was bringing a new enterprise, the cinema, there. Thus there was reason, on this visit, for the new air of authority I saw about him.

His friends did not see much of Joyce that second visit; he was out of Dublin, looking for theater sites in Belfast and

2 The mention of Joyce by Yeats is in three letters to Edmund Gosse, written in July 1915, asking that Joyce, then in Zurich, be considered eligible for a grant from the Royal Literary Fund, and in one letter to the secretary of that fund of about the same date, all in *The Letters of W. B. Yeats*, edited by Allan Wade (New York and London, 1954).

Cork, and when in the city he was busy supervising work in
Mary Street, reporting back to Trieste, getting out publicity
for this totally new enterprise. As regards the matter that was
closest to his heart, the publication of *Dubliners*, that did
not advance. The proofs, that were to have been given him
shortly after his arrival, were being held back. In the meantime the Volta Theatre opened, Dublin saw its first cinema,
and Joyce with something outside his own private mission
accomplished went back to Trieste.

Suppose it had been otherwise? Suppose that when he came
back to Dublin this time Joyce had walked into the publishers'
office and been handed the proofs of his first book? Suppose
he had gone back to Trieste with a small check on a Dublin
bank and a dozen copies of *Dubliners* in his trunk? What a
different impression he would have had of his native city!
Joyce would have been happier, of course; his mind would
have been free of the suspicion of persecution he was prone to.
But would there then have been a literature of exile?


## XI.  PADRAIC COLUM


As his treatment by Maunsel and Company at the time
of his second 1909 visit and afterward affected Joyce deeply,
and as he believed the episode had a secret history with which
I was *au courant* (I was not), I shall give some background
regarding it. I should remind the reader to begin with that at
the time Maunsel and Company were reputable publishers,
and that Joyce had an undertaking from them that the book
that was a major concern of his was on its way to publication.
In the course of the action I am about to relate the head of
Maunsels, George Roberts, will appear in a bad light. But as
he later came to regard the episode as a disastrous one in his
career, I shall try to present him sympathetically.

I knew George Roberts very well at a time when I knew
James Joyce only slightly. Like another poet I have mentioned,
James Cousins, Roberts was, to put it humorously, a refugee

from Belfast. Of Protestant and Unionist background (he was related in some degree to the British general, Lord Roberts, and bore some resemblance to him), he wanted to get to where there was some literary ferment, and had embraced the opportunity of settling in Dublin as a representative of a Belfast business. I used to go to his house where, with some other literary aspirants, I partook of teas and cakes that his mother grandly provided, and had stimulating readings and talks in his lamp-lit room. With the enthusiasm of our twenties we read *The Wanderings of Oisin* and talked about Nietzsche and Ibsen and prepared ourselves to take part in a revival of the Celtic spirit. George Roberts was a devoted "Meredithean," had editions of Meredith's poems and novels, and, with his eyes lighting, would read "The Lark Ascending," or, in more meditative fashion, "Melampus." He was older than I, perhaps twenty-seven or -eight to my twenty-three or -four, a stocky young man with blue eyes and blond hair that his fingers went through while he crowed with delight over a line in a poem or an exciting remark made by someone present.

That was the sympathetic side of George Roberts. But there was an unsympathetic side. He had moods in which he had a need to search for motives in people with whom he had pleasant relations; suspicions underlay his sunniness. As his bad temper took possession of him one could see his narrowed eyes looking round for the carving knife. There are people who study how to win friends and influence people; George Roberts knew how to lose friends and alienate people.

Like the rest of us who aspired to belong to the literary movement, George Roberts reached AE's Sunday evenings. His poems then appeared, with those of others of us, in a little collection AE edited, *New Songs*. Later we were all in the National Theatre Society, receiving tuition in verse-speaking, rehearsing plays, and attending conferences addressed by W. B. Yeats or George Moore, coming into contact with the pleasant but reserved John Synge. It was at a rehearsal of one of these early plays that James Joyce and George Roberts came together for the first time—not under good auspices, for that was the occasion I have recounted earlier, when Joyce was an intruder and when his legs carried him—

when he was invited to leave—no farther than the passageway, where he was stepped over by the Daughters of Ireland.

The stocky man with the Belfast accent, although he delighted in the speaking of poetry, did not seem to be material for an actor. But everyone in that mixed literary and theatrical group had to make some appearance on the stage, and George Roberts became one of the cast in Synge's *The Shadow of the Glen.* His was the part of the old farmer who feigns death in order to trap a suspected wife. I cannot say whether the part was well acted, but I still remember George Roberts standing beside the bed, a cudgel in his hand, vindictiveness in his face, and growling, "I've an ar-rum to me still," the Northern burr in his voice giving the words a peculiar significance.

As interest in the theater grew and an audience for published plays appeared, George Roberts graduated from doing odd jobs of publicity for the Society into regular publishing. Dublin was in need of a publisher with some literary standards; the ones in residence were in the educational or religious field, and, with few exceptions, all Irish literary work came out in London. George Roberts had a flair for the well-printed book and the good format, and when he set himself up as Maunsel and Company, it looked as if the Irish Revival had gained a practical outlet, a publishing house. When John Synge ended his brief career as a writer, Maunsels got the rights to his collected works and did a good job of bringing out the edition. But like everything progressive in Dublin at the time—the National Theatre, the Sinn Fein journal, the nationalist organizations—Maunsel and Company was undercapitalized. A young man who was a partner for a while did put some money into the firm, however.

So here was George Roberts, part literary man and part businessman, but mainly engaged in an effort to make a living wage for himself and a few employees, with Joyce's first serious work on his hands. The manuscript of *Dubliners* that Maunsel and Company contracted to publish for Joyce was more complete than the one that had finally been rejected by Grant Richards; the most memorable of the stories, "The Dead," had been added to it.

It should be said here that it was a bad time for the publication of books with realistic delineations in English-reading countries. In London, Grant Richards' printer censored some of Joyce's stories; in New York, a few years earlier, Dreiser's *Sister Carrie* had been turned back to the author after it had been set up in type. In London and Dublin the printers were aggressive, since libel actions were directed at them.

What made the Dublin publisher and printer behave even more scandalously about *Dubliners* in the end, than the London publisher had done? "It may be pointed out here," Herbert Gorman writes in his biography of Joyce,[1] expressing, no doubt, Joyce's own conviction, "that the printers were Falconer and Company, who did a lot of work for various Roman Catholic societies and were in a small way official printers to the Crown." Thus Joyce's biographer points to two alternatives —the Catholic societies and the Crown. As to the first, the ones that Joyce believed to be the real culprits, I can only say that in an association I later had with Falconers—somewhat after the time I am writing about they printed the *Irish Review*, of which I was editor—I never noticed any signs of business connected with Catholic societies. They were the last printing firm in Dublin I would have picked for a Catholic connection.

Falconers were known in literary history. The head of the firm at the time was lineally descended, I believe, from the Falconer who handled Jonathan Swift's manuscripts. He was the old-fashioned Dublin businessman, satisfied to make the thousand pounds a year that permitted him to have a villa in Killiney, the sort who was alarmed at any suggestion of business expansion and who kept any efficient man he might have as mere office help. In his spacious, shabby offices in O'Connell Street, where the main business was getting out a railway guide and timetable, in accordance with the deep-rooted idea of Dublin businessmen that no native was capable of running a business—which indeed was geared carefully to run itself— Falconer had a Scotsman as foreman, a good-humored fellow whom I remember for his braid Scots. Falconer himself was a neat, rosy-faced, elderly man who might have been the Caspar

[1] Herbert Gorman, *James Joyce*.

Milquetoast of the American comic strip—a tranquilized Caspar Milquetoast.

Joyce's later insistence that I had some knowledge of his affair with Maunsels (and so with Falconers) led me to examine my relations with Dublin printers, and I remembered an incident that in a slight way paralleled the suppression of *Dubliners*.

I was bringing out an issue of the *Irish Review*, which at that time was printed by Messrs. Manico. Going into the office one day, I asked young Mr. Manico, who appeared to be waiting for me, when the *Review* would be off the press. "I am sorry to say," he told me, "that we will have to change an article before the *Review* comes out." "What article?" He showed it to me: it was an article by Edward Martyn on the Feis Ceoil, the music festival, in which the remark was made that native music was being discriminated against by a board that was exclusively Masonic. Young Manico, speaking for his father, was very firm; the sentence about the Freemasons would have to be deleted or the *Review* would not come out that month. I went to Edward Martyn about it; he laughed. "I didn't really believe we would get it through," he said. As the sentence was only something in passing, he permitted me to delete it, and that issue of the *Irish Review* appeared.

Would a firm with the same connections as Manicos have printed *Dubliners*? No, because there was a reference to the royal patron of the Masonic Society. Over and over again, in the argument about publication, the reference to Edward VII in "Ivy Day in the Committee Room" was brought up. Joseph Hone, who was a member of the Maunsel firm at the time *Dubliners* was accepted, sees this reference as a key factor in Maunsels' and Falconers' refusal to publish. Here is the salient paragraph from Hone's article in the Joyce number of *Envoy* (April 1951):

*It was in 1908—the summer, I think—that I read Joyce's Dubliners in manuscript. The stories were written out in cheap notebooks in a copperplate hand that would have won for a schoolboy a prize in calligraphy. They were handed to me by George Roberts, the managing director of Maunsel*

*& Co., a publishing firm of which I was then a member.
Roberts was a very good judge of a book, beside being a fine
printer; but one, at least, of the stories gave him pause: such
is my recollection. This was "Ivy Day in the Committee
Room," in which Dublin's grave councillors are depicted in
discussing, among other matters, the private life of Edward
VII. As I look back, it occurs to me that the firm's hesitation,
as far as this particular story was concerned, may have been
due to a desire not to prejudice itself with Lady Aberdeen,
the then Lord Lieutenant's wife, by whom it had been commissioned to publish tracts relative to her anti-tuberculosis
campaign. But of this I am not certain.*

Though this may have been the overriding reason for the
refusal, it cannot have been the only one, for on this story
Joyce backed down. This I learned from a letter published in
*Sinn Fein*, a letter that Joyce had sent to all the Irish newspapers. In it there was a sentence that showed how worn out
Joyce was by his battles with prospective publishers of *Dubliners*. "I hereby give Messrs. Maunsel publicly permission to
publish this story ["Ivy Day in the Committee Room"] with
what changes or deletions they might please to make, and
shall hope that what they may publish may resemble that to
the writing of which I gave thought and time."

The letter is dated August 18, 1911. A year and a half had
gone by since Joyce had returned to Trieste, expecting the
proofs of the book momentarily. It was the first I knew that
Maunsels were not proceeding with the publication of *Dubliners* as, according to Joyce's reading of his contract with
them, they had obligated themselves to do.

## XII.   PADRAIC COLUM

The matter of *Dubliners* was still unsettled in the summer of 1912, when Joyce made another visit to Dublin. On
my first meeting with him on this occasion he was with Nora

(this was the first time I had met her) and he introduced me to her when I came over to them. Recently become a householder myself, I asked Joyce to visit my wife and me that evening. "Will there be any of the literati there?" he asked in the tone of one who had submitted to too many such trials. I got the impression that Nora wanted to come, but Joyce accepted the invitation perfunctorily—I having reassured him about the literati. My wife (as she has written here) had seen but not known Joyce at the university, and we both looked forward to having some time with him and Nora in our house. Then we received a telegram saying they were leaving Dublin for Galway that afternoon.

Sometime after this Joyce, returned from Galway, asked me to go with him to Maunsels' office. I found Roberts being sulky. I imagine that as a literary man he was ashamed of his conduct and as a publisher he was determined, contract or no contract, to get rid of *Dubliners*. His bad temper was probably aroused too. The tensions in his office might have been lightened if he had faced Joyce with something of his better nature and had said in his own idiom, "I'm bloody sorry, Joyce, but I did not know what I was letting myself in for when I passed your manuscript for publication. No matter what you cut out of it now, there would be actions that would ruin Maunsels."

As a matter of fact, Joyce's own solicitor had told him this. On my side, I had asked Tom Kettle, who was a lawyer, to read the proofs and tell me if Maunsel and Company were really in danger from libel actions; Kettle told me they were. But Roberts went on being sulky. His ugly attitude gave Joyce the sense of an enmity that was deep-seated and irrational. And there was Joyce, the proudest man in Dublin, asking this man not to condemn a book he had put so much into, and like any struggling author asking the whip-handed publisher to give him a break. "I will make deletions!" "I will cut out the story!" And still, refusal, refusal!

It went on in a meaningless way that afternoon—not an interview nor a consultation, but an argument that could get nowhere. What were the passages Roberts objected to? He kept going into and coming out of an inner office, consulting notes or conferring with somebody who stayed behind the scenes. I remember that the question of the naming of the public houses was raised. Joyce offered to take Roberts on a car with him, make the rounds of the pubs mentioned, and get an undertaking from each of their proprietors that no action would be taken because of a reference made to one or the other of them. Even this was refused.

Here were two badly situated men in a shabby office, with a third who was able to contribute very little. From it came effects on the two principals that made this a tragic action.[1] Years afterward, in London, I talked it all over with George Roberts. His great days as publisher to the Irish Renaissance were over; that they meant much to him was shown in the way he would speak to literary-minded men who might be present where we were: "Maunsel and Company, you know." He was then a "vanity" publisher and took the whole book-producing business in a cynical fashion. "I date my downfall from the Joyce affair," he said to me ruefully and penitently.

When I saw Roberts in Dublin (for the last time, as it turned out) a few years ago, I asked him to write out an account of his side of the wretched business. He told me he would, and I promised I'd have it published in an American journal. He never sent it, and now we are left to speculate as to whether or not there were any "dark forces" behind his and Falconers' outrageous conduct with regard to *Dubliners*. Joyce, as I have said, was always certain I had some inside information about it, and over and over again hinted I should disclose it; he expected I would do so in an introduction I was asked to write to the edition of *Dubliners* published in New York. But I hadn't then and I haven't now any such information.

It was gloomy parting with Joyce on that gloomy afternoon after the hopeless round in Maunsels' office. I had not been able to do anything to improve his position vis-à-vis his de-

[1] There is a classic irony in the fact that Joyce had even then laid up treasure for the George Roberts estate. In 1957 two letters from Joyce to Roberts—short notes written in the summer of 1904 when Joyce was trying to raise funds to go abroad with Nora, both asking for small sums of money: a total of 30 shillings in all—were sold at auction in London for 45 pounds. The sale, as reported in a Dublin newspaper, forms the *envoi* to that lamentable encounter.

faulting publisher, and Joyce was not going to make any polite pretense that I had. He said something about raising money to redeem the sheets, with the notion of bringing out the book himself somewhere. I had a feeling I was back in the days of *The Goblin*, George Webb's and Terence Kelly's. In spite of my having seen him in an affluent position, giving orders to Italian workmen in 1909, I knew that he knew that the cash to redeem the sheets was not available to him.

I saw him again, perhaps some weeks later, and this for the last time in Dublin. Somehow it got fixed in my mind that his brother Stanislaus was with him on this occasion, but this could not have been, for at the time Joyce was writing to him in Trieste. Some old-time follower, anyway, whom I mistook for Stanislaus joined in the conversation. There was still a question of Joyce's raising the money, getting the sheets back, and bringing out the book in London where he might get an advance from a publisher. A book of mine had just been published in London and I had had an advance of forty pounds. When I mentioned the amount Joyce looked significantly at the one whom I mistook for his brother, as if to say that forty pounds would be the crock of gold.

There and then I told him something that turned out to be helpful. "If you are in London and want somebody to help you with publishers, see a man named Ezra Pound," I told him. I gave him Pound's address. With the American he later made a contact that led to a friendship which lasted until *Work in Progress*, which Pound did not approve of, began publication. Joyce was to say to me, speaking of Pound long afterward, "He took me out of the gutter."

Joyce managed to secure one set of proofs of *Dubliners*, but Falconers burned the sheets rather than deliver them to the author or to another publisher, thereby losing the chance of getting paid for them. But before receiving this kick on the shins from the printers, Joyce had been dealt this kick behind by his publishers: "They [Maunsels' legal advisers] advise that the author has committed a breach of guarantee contained in clause eleven," George Roberts had the gall to write Joyce, "by offering for publication a book which as he should know is clearly libellous; and they recommend, if I so desire, that

Maunsel and Company proceed against you in order to re-
cover all costs, charges and expenses for time, labour and
materials expended on the book. . . . I must ask you to make
a substantial offer towards covering our loss. Failing your doing that I shall have most reluctantly to put the matter in
other hands."

Thus the author's hopes about his first serious work were
almost maniacally destroyed. Returning to Trieste, he would
find himself again going from one end of the city to the other
to give lessons to private pupils, and struggling to hold a portion of his day for the revision of *Stephen Hero* that would
make it *Portrait of the Artist*, or for the writing of his play or
for the development of a short story he had in his mind—the
story of a Dublin day, which was to become *Ulysses*. *Dubliners*, the publication of which would have meant a possible
margin on which to do this writing, had been flung back at
him, and Joyce saw in its rejection evidence that occult forces
were arrayed against him. For the land in which these forces
had established themselves there was no hope, and his vale-
dictory, at this final parting from Ireland, was barbed with
his contempt:

> *This lovely land that always sent*
> *Her writers and artists to banishment*
> *And in a spirit of Irish fun*
> *Betrayed her own leaders, one by one,*
> *'Twas Irish humour, wet and dry,*
> *Flung quicklime into Parnell's eye.*

## XIII. PADRAIC COLUM

The Joyce whom I spoke to that last afternoon, when the
only assistance I could offer him was the name of a man in
London, was a Joyce now going into exile in earnest. True,
he was going back to a city he had been at home in for a
significant part of his life, where he had a wife and two chil-

dren, not to speak of a brother and sister who had joined him there; he was going back to a place where there were people who were congenial to him. Why, then, did this particular departure come to be marked by him as an unmitigated exile? There is testimony that it was. Years afterward, with his friend the Triestine novelist Italo Svevo, he was present at a performance of his play in London. " 'Exiled?' I asked him," says Svevo. " 'Exiled? People who return to their home country!' 'But don't you remember,' said Joyce to me, 'how the prodigal son was received by his brother in his father's house. It is dangerous to leave one's country, but still more dangerous to go back to it, for then your fellow-countrymen, if they can, will drive a knife into your heart.' "[1]

It is from the time of this departure from Dublin in 1912 that the word "exile" in the sense of "banishment," "proscription," comes to be used by Joyce as something that evokes all one's spiritual powers and by doing so leads to creativeness. "I go to encounter for the millionth time the reality of experience and to forge in the smithy of my soul the uncreated conscience of my race." That was not said by the Stephen Hero whose book was written in Dublin, but by the Stephen Dedalus who after his final departure from Ireland transformed that book. True, *Stephen Hero* as we have it is incomplete, but the personage in that novel is no artificer.

The Joyce from whom I parted at the corner of what was then called Brunswick Street in Dublin had only one book to his credit, *Chamber Music*, and that book had got only one review—by Arthur Symons. In Joyce's possession was a single unbound copy of a collection of short stories that a Dublin printer and a Dublin publisher had let him have from under their counter. In Trieste was the manuscript of a novel no part of which had the detachment nor the distinction of some of the stories in this rejected book. The Joyce who stood with me and a companion that afternoon was not yet the Joyce whom a public was to acclaim—he was just "Jimmie" Joyce, who had the distinction of having been abroad and of having brought a Continental form of entertainment to Dublin.

This time Dublin had literally rejected him. Here, crowding

[1] Italo Svevo, *James Joyce*.

the streets, were the men and women in whose name the rejection had been made, the men and women "engaged," as he
had written, "in the conspiracy of ignobility." George Roberts
and George Falconer were the agents of that rejection, and
behind them were the faceless giants of the church and state.
This was the last time he would see with the outer eye the
clouded skies, the river, the sea gulls hovering above the gray
houses, the green that was his—Stephen's Green—the gray shaft
of the Nelson monument, the pillars before the General
Post Office.

But was not this return to Dublin, this manhandling by
Roberts and Falconer, this quenching of a hope that had
given him so much elation, the fulfillment of a destiny? We
listen to the Stephen Dedalus of *Ulysses* discuss the ways of
the artist. . . . "John Eglinton looked in the tangled glow-
worm of his lamp. —The world believes that Shakespeare
made a mistake, he said, and got out of it as quickly and as
best he could. —Bosh! Stephen said rudely. A man of genius
makes no mistakes. His errors are volitional and are the portals
of discovery." This return to Dublin, then, this traffic with
printers and publishers were not mistakes—they had sharpened his eyes to look on a people and a city as no one before
had looked on them, they had cleared his ears to hear the
murmurs of the city, the speech of the citizens. . . . "—He
found in the world without as actual what was in his world
within as possible. Maeterlinck says: *If Socrates leave his
house today he will find the sage seated on his doorstep. If
Judas go forth tonight it is to Judas his steps will tend.*"

Joyce went back to Trieste with his single copy of *Dubliners*
—back to the bread-earning grind. But as in his going and
coming from University College he could, shutting out the
external scene, give himself to the selection of words and images. Walking across an Italian city, climbing stairs to give
lessons, approaching "midway in this our mortal life," Joyce
must have felt himself taking steps with the poet whose
Comedy was formed by exile. An inner mutation had in any
case taken place. In Trieste *Stephen Hero* was not revised,
rewritten, reconstructed—it was transformed, to appear as *A
Portrait of the Artist as a Young Man*. The dialectician had
become the revealer of the epiphany. And the passage from

dialectic to epiphany is the significant one in the life of James Joyce the artist.

Dialectic is communication in *Stephen Hero*. In *Portrait of the Artist* there is a scene in which one can see this dialectic becoming epiphany. Stephen and his friend Cranly, walking together, discuss Stephen's loss of faith. At the end of a give-and-take Stephen answers: "—What kind of a liberation would that be to forsake an absurdity which is logical and coherent and embrace one which is illogical and incoherent?" Then:

*They had walked on towards the township of Pembroke and now, as they went on slowly along the avenues, the trees and the scattered lights in the villas soothed their minds. The air of wealth and repose diffused about them seemed to comfort their neediness. Behind a hedge of laurel a light glimmered in the window of a kitchen and the voice of a servant was heard singing as she sharpened knives. She sang, in short broken bars,* Rosie O'Grady.

*Cranly stopped to listen, saying:*

—Mulier cantat.

*The soft beauty of the Latin word touched with an enchanting touch the dark of the evening, with a touch fainter and more persuading than the touch of music or of a woman's hand. The strife of their minds was quelled. The figure of a woman as she appears in the liturgy of the church passed silently through the darkness: a white robed figure, small and slender as a boy, and with a falling girdle. Her voice, frail and high as a boy's, was heard intoning from a distant choir the first words of a woman which pierce the gloom and clamour of the first chanting of the passion:*

—Et tu cum Jesu Galilaeo eras.

*And all hearts were touched and turned to her voice, shining like a young star, shining clearer as the voice intoned the proparoxyton and more faintly as the cadence died.*

*The singing ceased. They went on together, Cranly repeating in strongly stressed rhythm the end of the refrain:*

> And when we are married,
>    O, how happy we'll be
> For I love sweet Rosie O'Grady,
>    And Rosie O'Grady loves me.

# II. PARIS

# I.   MARY M. COLUM

In 1919, just after the end of World War I, my husband received a letter from Joyce saying he was in dire need of a thousand dollars. We were then living in New York, and the Joyces were in Zurich, where they had gone at the outbreak of war to avoid internment in Trieste. The income Joyce had from giving English lessons had proved inadequate in Switzerland, and though he had received some temporary aid from Mrs. Harold McCormick, a daughter of John D. Rockefeller who was then in Switzerland, and later more substantial help from Miss Harriet Weaver, his lifelong benefactress, his situation was still not easy. Near the end of the war he had become involved in a venture to produce plays in English in Zurich. Out of this had come some sort of run-in with the British consul in the Swiss city, and his present money difficulties.

Joyce wrote, at the same time he did to us, to Benjamin Huebsch, the American publisher of *Dubliners* and *Portrait of the Artist*, and Huebsch managed to get together a couple of hundred dollars; to raise more than that was not easy in America, when it was for a writer few people had then heard of.

My husband and I had no talent for raising money, but I did have one good idea. At that time the reconstituted *Dial* was edited by a young man I had met, Scofield Thayer. Parts of Joyce's *Ulysses* had been appearing in America in the *Little Review*, and Thayer had written about them in an understanding way. He was rich enough to subsidize the *Dial*, and so I thought he might contribute to the Joyce fund. I telephoned him and, lacking courage to tell him on the phone what I wanted, asked him to come to see us. We were living at the time on West Seventy-ninth Street.

Thayer was there in twenty minutes, and we began to tell him about Joyce's case. At my husband's request I read aloud Joyce's letter. I can never forget Scofield Thayer's sympathy. "Don't try to collect anything yourselves," he said. "It will only harass you. I will give the money." His generosity touched me very much.

My husband and I returned to Ireland in 1921, the year *Ulysses* came out. I was asked to review the book for the American magazine *The Freeman*, then edited by Albert Jay Nock, with Van Wyck Brooks as literary editor. Brooks was absent at the time I sent my review, so it went to Nock. The opening sentence was a harmless enough remark to the effect that within the next couple of decades many books would be published on Joyce and *Ulysses*. Nock wrote me an annoyed letter saying he was deleting these lines, as they would have been an exaggeration if applied to Cervantes or Tolstoi on the publication of any of their works. But later he was fond of quoting publicly a version of that sentence, and of saying how right I had been.

My review was one of three that came out in America that Joyce liked (the other two were by Edmund Wilson and Gilbert Seldes, bright young critics of that day), and though I had known him only by sight in Dublin years before, he sent me a cable when he read it. We were in Paris the following autumn, and had hoped to see Joyce, but he was away in the south of France. He telegraphed from there, when he heard we were in Paris, asking us to wait for his return, but as we were due in the Hawaiian Islands in a few weeks we could not stay.

Two years later, again in Paris, I met Joyce face to face for the first time. On our way to where they lived, we turned a corner and saw two persons coming our way. My husband recognized them as Joyce and Nora. He called, "Joyce," and when Joyce looked up I realized he was nearly sightless. I think it was Nora who recognized my husband. They were on their way to keep some appointment, but Joyce seemed eager to see us, and they asked us to dinner at their apartment that evening.

## PADRAIC COLUM

I was curious, on that first visit to Joyce in Paris, to see what changes his long stay away from Ireland had made in him. I noticed a Greek flag on the wall of the vestibule of his apartment. "The Greeks have always brought me good luck," he said when I looked inquiringly at it. The flag, he told me, was a relic of Trieste. In that Mediterranean seaport he had spoken to Greeks and learned the Greek vernacular.

There, too, he had made a close friend, the novelist I have mentioned who wrote under the name of Italo Svevo, but whose real name was Schmitz: he was of Jewish origin, as was his wife. That their friendship meant much to the Joyces was shown by the fact that in the apartment in Paris, in later years, the portrait of Madame Schmitz—a kindly-looking older woman—occupied a place of honor.

The Hellene and the Semite! Perhaps it was in Trieste that Victor Bérard's discoveries came home to Joyce: that the Semites were first in the Mediterranean, that they named the islands, and that it was their language that the poet of the Odyssey knew as the language of the gods. Odysseus and the Wandering Jew were different versions of the same character. In Dublin the then-untraveled Joyce had spoken to me of the Greek epics as being outside European culture: he used to say that the *Divine Comedy* was Europe's epic. It must have been by the Mediterranean that he realized that the first artificer was a Mediterranean man, and it was then that Stephen Hero became Stephen Dedalus.

But in Trieste he had found not only the strange but the familiar. When I recalled to him, in Paris, that Stendhal had been consul in Trieste, he said, "Charles Lever was consul there too," speaking as if that was something of import. With his habit of seeking out intellectual landmarks wherever he settled, Joyce had turned up a record in Trieste of an Irish resident. Charles Lever was a nineteenth-century Irish novelist, author of such books as *Charles O'Malley, the Irish Dragoon* and *Arthur O'Leary: his wanderings and ponderings in many lands*—books which I doubt if Joyce ever read.

## MARY M. COLUM

We were the only guests at the Joyces' that first evening; their son Giorgio was not at home, but their daughter Lucia was. She was a pretty young girl, diffident, it seemed to me, speaking seldom and then in Italian to her father or mother. The odd way her eyes were set was noticeable, but did not prevent her from being attractive-looking. I wondered how long it had been since Joyce had written that poem about her that I had read in *Poetry*:

> O bella bionda,
> Sei come l'onda!

> A *moondew stars her hanging hair*
> *And moonlight kisses her young brow*
> *And, gathering, she sings an air:*
> *Fair as the wave is, fair, art thou!*

Nora Joyce wore a scarlet shawl that set off her abundant graying hair, fine eyes, and good features. She spoke of the great lift the money sent them in Zurich by Scofield Thayer had given them. "It was a godsend," she said, and Joyce said very earnestly that the gift had saved him at the moment; the troubles connected with the theatrical venture had been such, we gathered, as would have oppressed a more equable spirit than his. Nora told an amusing story about that dolorous time. A sum of money (either that from Thayer or some help they received after it) had arrived one day when Joyce was out at a rehearsal. Nora, all excitement, went over to the theater where, before all the company rehearsing, she informed her husband of their luck. Joyce was so overcome he said little, but in the midst of the congratulations from the company the wife of one of the actors turned to Nora and said, with an edge in her voice, "And so, Mrs. Joyce, you open your husband's letters."

Nora Joyce, as I came to see as I knew her better, was not only beautiful but vivacious and humorous. Though she had but little education, she had natural aptitudes, among them a love and understanding of music. She and Joyce could be together in the realm of music, though—I later found out—she had little comprehension of literature, and none at all of the sort of literature Joyce produced. She and I talked, that evening, chiefly of clothes and hats.

James Joyce was markedly devoted to Nora; her personality was full of interest to him, and he delighted in her sayings and snappy remarks. Once, when I called to see Nora, I found Joyce crumpled up in delight at something she was saying. She had just come from Sylvia Beach's bookshop on the rue de l'Odéon—where "Lo and behold! There was Miss Beach nursing a headache and looking like a wild Electra." And again, speaking of the somewhat slummy apartment a writer friend used as a *pied-à-terre*, she said: "That place is not fit to wash a rat in."

She had a very odd name—Nora Barnacle. In some way that I can't remember Joyce connected her family with one that had a Norman name—Mortimer. "Death at sea," Joyce noted. To him, who had such a feeling for "correspondences" between names and lives, this meant something. He was quite serious about it.

Nora had been brought up in a convent in Galway town, but I always believed it was in the orphanage side of the convent. In talking to me about her early surroundings she mentioned that she had been sent through the town with messages, by the nuns. This could not have happened if she had been a boarder or a day pupil at the convent. Also her attitude toward the sisters was different from that a pupil who had been trained by them would have had: Nora had not the least respect or affection for them, but rather suspicion and hostility.

Yet it was rather unlikely that Nora had been taken into the convent because her family was poverty-stricken. Her uncle, Michael Healy, whom Joyce respected, had been well enough off to help the young couple from time to time, and enough of a man of the world to have Joyce present him with his books as they were published. Nora had no skills, or none that I ever noticed—which also indicates that she might have been brought up by nuns in an orphanage. I never put much stock in her having been, as people said, working behind the bar counter in one of the Dublin hotels at the time Joyce met her. It was just the most likely thing for Dublin gossips to say after her elopement with Joyce.

I noticed on this first meeting something I was to remark again and again about Joyce—his solicitude for his friends. There had been a report of a tidal wave in the Hawaiian Islands, where we had been, and Joyce, although he had not seen us before we went to the Pacific, had been anxious about us.

After dinner we sat and talked in another room. We spoke about *Ulysses*, my husband, I remember, asking Joyce why he had turned the chaste Penelope into Molly Bloom. Joyce justified the change in some way, quoting some Greek writer I had never heard of as an authority for making Penelope less than virtuous. (About that monologue of Molly Bloom's the psychologist C. G. Jung wrote in very Teutonic English, "I think the devil's grandmother knows as much about the psychology of a woman—I don't. . . . It is a string of psychological peaches.")

After a time Joyce said to Nora, "Do you think the Colums would like to hear that new thing of mine?" The Colums assured him that they would. Then and there he read to us—and we may have been the first to hear his reading of it—what has come to be known as *Anna Livia Plurabelle*.

As yet there had been no intimation of what the successor to *Ulysses* was to be, and now we were having a first view of it. I listened fascinated to the flow of words in Joyce's melodious and changing voice. I confess I thought him more of a musician than a writer in this venture of his. But he read so earnestly and beautifully that the invocation in the piece grew and grew as he went on.

And so we had our initiation into what we were to discuss as *Work in Progress* and to read years later as *Finnegans Wake*. We talked about the piece, and Joyce showed his delight as one or the other of us picked up references that only inhabitants of the city or the countryside of the Liffey would spot. He told us the number of names of rivers he had worked into the episode—two hundred, I think, and this was only his first draft: he was to add to them. He had written it, he told us, on an upturned portmanteau in some hotel where they were waiting to get rooms.

I don't recall that we saw the Joyces on any other occasion during our stay in Paris that year.

## II. PADRAIC COLUM

Our third visit to Paris, after the end of World War I, was in 1927, the fifth year of *Ulysses*. We saw more of Joyce this time than on the previous visit.

I should say here that the chronology of our sojourns in Paris during the late 1920's and early 1930's is something of a tangled skein. It is probable that encounters my wife and I had with the Joyces that were later than others will be written of as prior, and the other way around. I am depending, in my part, upon my memory, which is a lively one. And where character, incident, and speech are the important things, chronology does not so much matter.

In 1927 Joyce's *Work in Progress* had begun to appear in the newly launched magazine *transition*, and was being hailed, explained, shrugged off. The furor over *Ulysses* continued, meanwhile, and its author had become the most talked-of writer in Europe, interest in him extending as far as the Vatican. Joyce was now a man of mark.

Headquarters in Paris for all that had to do with Joyce was the Shakespeare Head Bookshop, in the rue de l'Odéon. This was the shop owned by Miss Sylvia Beach, the American woman who, with her partner, Adrienne Monnier, had published *Ulysses*. I went into the shop soon after our arrival in Paris, on this visit, and found Miss Beach—small, smiling, and with that beautiful voice that Joyce often drew attention to—in a welcoming mood. She had the elation of one who finds herself in a worthy, exciting, and wholly satisfactory venture. As publisher of *Ulysses*, which, though banned, was selling numerous copies to pilgrims who came to the bookshop, Miss

Beach patently recognized her good fortune in being able to forward Joyce's interests.

Mr. Joyce would certainly be glad to see me, Miss Beach said, and saying this, she went to the telephone to call him and let him know I was actually there. I spoke to him then myself, and he invited my wife and me to dinner with him that evening at Les Trianons, his then-favorite restaurant.

Beside the magnitudinous *Ulysses* there was now in Miss Beach's shop a little volume by James Joyce entitled *Pomes Penyeach*. A word for "apples" was imposed on "poems" in the title, giving the sense of windfalls bought at a wayside stall. These same forms of imposition were being lavishly used in *Work in Progress*. As the price of the little volume was a shilling, one expected to find twelve poems in it, one for each penny. Actually there were thirteen, the additional one being named "Tilly." In this Joyce was being obscurely local: the extra half-cup of milk that the milkman left in the Dublin householder's jug in the morning was a "tilly"—something unpaid for. This small collection was the first poetic one Joyce had published since *Chamber Music*. It had its own color. *Chamber Music* had had the light of day; *Pomes Penyeach* were all night pieces, some with the blackness and oppression of night, some with night's quietude. I was told that as *Ulysses* was of the day, *Work in Progress* would be of the night. If that were so, *Pomes Penyeach* had foreshadowed the change. Still, there was a good deal of night life in *Ulysses*.

Joyce, I learned on this visit, had acquired not only admirers but friends—he was surrounded by a whole tribe of devoted friends, for whom the bookshop was a center of operations. Several of the friends gave practical help on *Work in Progress*, for Joyce's eyes, operated on frequently and painfully, were not equal to long periods of close work. The actual writing of the text was done by Joyce on long strips of paper—sometimes cardboard—with different colored crayons. But the setting up of the cryptic language, the corrections, and the many revisions on the proofs necessitated a great deal of supervision that could not all be given by Joyce.

Among the helpers and friends were Eugene Jolas, founder and editor of *transition*, and his wife Maria, who had been trained as an opera singer and with whom Joyce shared wide

musical interests—she was a rich-natured person. There was
Stuart Gilbert, a humorous Englishman who, retired from a
judgeship in Burma, was making himself an authority on the
arcana of *Ulysses,* on which he later published a commentary,
and on the deeper mysteries of *Work in Progress;* there was
Gilbert's charming French wife Moune. A most devoted
helper, acquired a little after this time, was Paul Léon.

There was also Herbert Gorman, who was writing Joyce's
biography.

The staff of the bookshop were Joyce's helpers too, in a
sense. Assisting Miss Beach there was a Greek young lady,
Miss Moschos, dignified and intelligent. Miss Moschos, I remember, had a sister, a young girl who was very hushed and
very retiring: she came forward only to deliver mail or bring
proofs to Joyce. I am glad to remember that the most diffident
of Joyce's helpers had a tribute from him:

> *Little Miss Moschos*
> *Soft as a mouse goes*

But I can't recall the rest of the verse.

Along with these I've named there were several other persons, men and women, all enthusiastic about Joyce's work
and Joyce's personality. They were all intelligent and charming people, in no wise given to speaking with bated breath of
"the master," but happy to be close to one who was not only
a celebrity but a likable and entertaining man. I believe there
is none of them but looks back to those early days in the Joyce
orbit as being particularly happy ones.

As Joyce's was a work in progress, mine in regard to it
became an enlightenment in progress. How did I get to know
what *Work in Progress* was about?

As I went for walks with Joyce in the afternoons I attempted
to make landings on and explorations of the territory that was
looming before us. Joyce suggested I should read Vico. But
had Vico been translated into a language I could read? Yes,
Michelet had translated him into French. That was not too
easy for me either, and I decided I could get enough knowledge of Vico to pass by reading the article about him in the

*Encyclopaedia Britannica.* Meanwhile I could talk about him on our promenades.

"He was one of those round-headed Neapolitan men," Joyce told me. I forget whom he mentioned as another of them. He told me of Vico's theory of cycles in history. These historical cycles connected in some way with the Vico Road that follows the bend of Dublin Bay between Dalkey and Killiney—in Joyce's mind they did, anyway.

When I read the article on Vico in the *Britannica* I knew that I already had some familiarity with his ideas, at third or fourth hand. I felt as I did when I identified some commonplace of a geography lesson with the genius of Von Humboldt. What was Vico's view of that work in progress which is human history? First, that great racial figures such as Romulus were the summing up of historical happenings and had themselves no historical existence. Then, that history proceeds from the Cyclops in his cave to Achilles on the battlefield to Caesar in his tent to Nero in his palace and begins again with the Cyclops in his cave. History is cyclic, and the general scheme of *Work in Progress* was to be cyclic—it would start from where it had left off, or rather, its beginning and end would be continuous. The Cyclops, Achilles, Caesar, Nero, would all be resumed in one figure—H.C.E., Here Comes Everybody. "Of course," Joyce told me, "I don't take Vico's speculations literally; I use his cycles as a trellis."

Joyce went back to Vico as to a writer who had some authority in the world of European thought. But there was a line of Irish thinkers and artists he could have gone back to— Johannes Scotus Erigena and the artist of the Book of Kells, a reproduction of which he often turned to. Here was the cyclic world-view at its most elaborate. "In Ireland," wrote Henri Focillon in his *The Life of Forms in Art,* "the interlace appears as a transitory, but endlessly renewed meditation on a chaotic universe that deep within itself clasps and conceals the debris or the seeds of humankind. The interlace turns round and round the old iconography and devours it. It creates a picture of the world that has nothing in common with the world, and an art of thinking that has nothing in common with thought."

A picture of the world that has nothing in common with

the world and an art of thinking that has nothing in common
with thought! Could what Joyce was doing in *Work in Progress* be taken in this sense? Sometimes as we walked together
Joyce would make some casual statement that would show
his thinking was on another level altogether from that which
the majority of us cultivated. The four old men who exchange
remarks in some episodes of *Work in Progress*—they were the
Four Evangelists, weren't they? Yes, or the Four Masters—
they being the scholars who compiled the annals of Ireland.
And so the number four could be associated, I thought, with
the recording or the handing down of matters. But the four
were also the four provinces of Ireland, Joyce informed me.
Or the four ingredients in a salad. And so my guess about
four being the number of a recording was not a valid one.
The number twelve seemed to have a firmer status. "Twelve is
the public number," Joyce told me. "Twelve hours of the day,
twelve men on a jury."

Later I found that in any system I shaped I would have to
leave a place for the casual or the arbitrary. For instance, in
*Finnegans Wake*, page 552, there is a brilliant description of
the cathedral H.C.E. builds before his downfall. It is Saint
Patrick's in Dublin, but it is also the older Christ church.
The sounding bell, the colors of the windows, the peal of the
organ become one—it is a triumph of that simultaneity that
Joyce's later technique is directed toward. History is present
too. One of the Norse kings of Dublin desecrated the altar of
Christ church by having his wife sit naked on it, and thus
the "chillybombom . . . upon the altarstane." Telfords were
the organ makers in Dublin, and so we have the anthem "to
tellforth's glory" (but only a local boy would know that). How
amusing the episode is, not only for the "chillybombom" but
also for the evocation of that Sunday-morning hurriedness as
the bell rings for Mass—"massgo bell" with its overtone of
"Moscow"—to "commind the fitful":

. . . *her paddypalace on the crossknoll with massgo bell, six-
ton clashcloshant, duominous and muezzatinties to commind
the fitful: doom adimdim adoom adimadim: and the oragel of
the lauds to tellforth's glory: and added thereunto a shallow
laver to slub out her hellfire and posied windows for her oriel*

*house: gospelly pewmillieu, christous pewmillieu: zackbutts*
*babazounded, ollguns tararulled: and she sass her nach, chilly-*
*bombom and forty bonnets, upon the altarstane.*

But what is "forty bonnets" doing there? Whatever their significance, a particularly charming sentence has its rhythm
broken by them.

Those forty bonnets are a memento of Miss Rebecca West.
She came to Paris, bought a copy of *Chamber Music* and one
of *Ulysses,* and then made a professional assay of Joyce's
achievement. Reading *Chamber Music,* she decided that the
verse was sentimental, and passing on to *Ulysses* she found a
like sentimentality in its pages. James Joyce was a camouflaged
sentimentalist. And having given this verdict, Miss West announced that she was going out to buy herself a bonnet.

Now, "she sass her nach, chillybombom upon the altarstane" is fine, but "she sass her nach, chillybombom and forty
bonnets, upon the altarstane" has neither grace nor continuity.
Joyce is arbitrary here. But I have no doubt that bonnets are
worked into the cycles: they are likely to be associated with
any extra woman's part. And just as twelve is a public number
and four is—shall we say—a unifying number, forty denotes
frivolousness: the frivolousness of women who go off to buy
bonnets after making snap judgments on books of manifold
significance.

But if the Norse king's wife entered the historical cycles
by sitting down on the altar stone of Christ church, others
who had no claim even on newspaper notice entered them
too. Reminiscing with the composer of *Work in Progress,* I
spoke of being in a Dublin music hall, the Lyric (or was it
the Tivoli?), when a gang of students ragged a female performer by tossing at her feet a large corset. She made an indignant rejoinder, declaring she was a Dublin girl and entitled
to decent treatment from Dublin fellows. Maybe it was *be-*
*cause* she was a Dublin girl—residence might have set up a
score against her—that there was the immodest demonstration.
I didn't think that anyone except myself remembered it, and
I remembered it because it was the first and last time I was
among what was for me the far from respectable audience of
that particular music hall. But Joyce hadn't missed it. With

the triumph of a historian who has made a footnote to one
of Gibbon's footnotes, he exclaimed: "I have her in. She is
the one who is madjealous." The performer's name was
Madge Ellis. So there it is. And if I didn't make it public,
would the best equipped commentator ever be able to reveal
what is behind that "madjealous" in *Finnegans Wake?*

The curious affinities words had with things were often remarked on by Joyce as we took our walks. I recall a couple
of instances. A passing bus had for its terminal Gobelins. The
place name suggested "goblins." And how right that was, for
the figures on the tapestries were goblin-like. Again, two men,
one of them obviously hard of hearing, were trying to converse
as we went by. The word often used for "deafness" in Ireland
is "bothered" (it comes from the Irish word for "deaf"). Joyce
noted this and commented on its rightness—a deaf man is a
"bothered" man.

Once Nora had decreed that "Jim" was to get himself a
new suit, and the three of us took a taxi to a shop near the
Galeries Lafayette. Even while trying on pants and jackets
under the scrutiny of his wife Joyce was not completely detached from *Work in Progress.* He laughed like a schoolboy
who has inserted a meaningful cipher on the margin of his
lessons when I told him I had identified the "Tantrist" of
one of the installments in *transition*: he is Tristan the trickster,
the one who leaps backward from Iseult's bed. "I don't know
how I can think of such things," he said, as though delighted
with himself.

We passed a bird shop the sign of which was the effigy of a
medieval saint. Joyce and I identified him as Saint Fiacre,
and we recalled the time when the hired vehicle on these
streets was the fiacre. What was the connection between the
saint and the vehicle? Well, centuries before, the saint had a
well-cultivated garden outside the town, and people with a
holiday to spend would say, "Let's go to Fiacre's garden." And
Fiacre himself, we are told, was the son of the King of Scotland. But "Scotland" as the name for a country did not exist
in Fiacre's time: "Scot" was the Latin for "Gael" and specifi-
cally for "Irishman." So Fiacre emerged as the Irish Fiacra
who was probably one of the scholars at the court of Charles

the Bald. And here he was now, once the patron of gardens, now the patron of birds of the garden.

History as transmitted in this way fascinated Joyce: it was not outside but inside ourselves. Some particle of the influence of those misnamed men who spoke Latin with an Irish accent to the Carlovingian kings must still be present among the millions of other influences, he reflected, must even exist in the minds of people on the street that morning. And the history that lies below our intellectual preoccupations is a theme in *Work in Progress*.

## III.   MARY M. COLUM

*Work in Progress* continued to progress in *transition*. About this time we were invited to a reading Joyce gave in his apartment of parts of the book, including *Anna Livia Plurabelle*. An alert audience was present, Hemingway among them; only a few French writers were there. As he proceeded with his reading Joyce threw an occasional glance at his listeners. He fixed it on me at one passage, adding to my confusion: although I had heard him read from the *Work* before, I had not arrived at any real comprehension of it.

When the reading, made memorable by his beautiful voice, was over, Joyce stood before me for a moment or two, and I shook in my shoes. "Well?" he questioned. "What do you think?" I summoned my courage up and answered with what I fear was pomposity: "Joyce, I think it is outside literature." He fastened his eyes on me, making no response. I do not know what the others present said when he spoke to them, but I gathered later that they did not say anything that showed enlightenment. In fact, I believe speeches more pompous than mine were handed out—an allocution by Elliot Paul and some observations by Robert McAlmon.

It was a month before my husband and I saw Joyce again, for we went to Switzerland. My husband went to see him on our return. Joyce seemed to have spent some time chewing over the comments his audience had handed out to him. Right away he leaped on mine. "Your wife," he said sternly, "said that what I read was outside literature. Tell her it may be outside literature now, but its future is inside literature."

However, he did not hold my judgment against me, and when, later, Robert McAlmon wrote in a book that he entitled *Being Geniuses Together* that I had had to pretend to understand what Joyce read on account, he said, of my "position as an intellectual critic," Joyce said to me with his delightful smile: "But you were the only one present who frankly said you did not understand it. I remember how you laughed at passages that were humorous—that was more than any of the others did."

At that time the Abbé Jousse was lecturing in Paris. He was a noted propounder of a theory that Joyce gave adherence to, that language had its origin in gesture—"In the beginning was the rhythmic gesture," Joyce often said. Joyce invited me to go with him to a lecture the Abbé was giving. It was in a small hall, and Joyce, I thought, went toward our seats with a remarkable uncertainty. An attendant came to us, and murmurs went round the coterie kind of audience: "M'sieu James Joyce! M'sieu James Joyce!" Attention was centered on Joyce—to his satisfaction, I believe.

If the Abbé's lecture did not interest me as much as it interested Joyce, still, it interested me a great deal, and that largely because of its original method of presentation. It took the form of a little play, based on the Gospels. Around the lecturer was a group of girls, who addressed him as "Rabbi Jesus." The words spoken—one of the parables, I think—were, I gathered, in Aramaic, and what was shown was that the word was shaped by the gesture. Joyce was full of the subject and talked to me about the lecture as we went along to the café where my husband was waiting for us, but I can't remember what he said.

Joyce was talking very earnestly to the two of us in the café when I noticed a young man who had followed us from the lecture hall hovering near. Joyce could not omit a piece of blasphemy when mentioning a heavenly gesture. Then he got onto something else that caught my husband's attention. It was about the improvement algebra had made in our way of numbering, a few x's and y's taking the place of cumbersome rows of figures. "The equation in mathematics and the syllogism in logic are the great intellectual inventions," Joyce declared.

The young man who had followed us—he was an American, of course—asked if he might be allowed to sit with us for a few minutes. He turned out to be an instructor in literature, and was eager to gather information from Joyce in person about the technical inventions in *Ulysses*. Joyce was now in the mood for a characteristic leg-pull.

In an interview after *Ulysses* was published, Joyce had informed a credulous public that he got the whole idea of the interior monologue from the old French novelist Edouard Dujardin, who had monologues of some kind in a novel called *Les Lauriers Sont Coupés*. Dujardin was extremely happy at being resurrected: the author of the great modern literary creation had acknowledged indebtedness to him, who had not been heard of for a generation. A new edition of his forgotten novel was issued, with a dedication to Joyce. To the young college instructor from America Joyce now began handing out the Dujardin-influence line; full of good spirits, he made it so luxuriant that the young man drew out a notebook into which he scribbled furiously what he was being told.

After he left I said to Joyce, "Haven't you had enough fun with this? Haven't you pulled enough people's legs? And why deny your indebtedness to Freud and Jung? Isn't it better to be indebted to great originators like that than to . . . ?" He stopped me, evidently angry, and moving irritatedly in his chair. "I hate women who know anything," he said. "No, Joyce, you don't," I said. "You like them." After a few seconds of silent annoyance, a whimsical smile came over his face, and the rest of the afternoon was pleasant for the three of us.

Joyce could not be broken of his leg-pulling addiction, however. Once several years later when I was with him and when, Nora not being present, he had managed to get drunk, he told me that he had had his grandson named Stephen because that was the name of Freud's grandson. "Do you think you are talking to a simpleton?" I exclaimed. "Your grandson, we all know, had to be called after Stephen Dedalus. No more of this, by Godesse dignitee," I added, echoing Chaucer.

But one had to know Joyce personally to know when the leg-pulling was on. I remember being at dinner at the Joyces' when, in the middle of the meal, Thomas McGreevy, now head of the National Gallery of Ireland, telephoned to say he was dropping in later with a friend. Joyce fell into consternation; the addition of two more would bring the number of guests up to thirteen. Those present who did not know him well thought it an elaborate joke when he began driving us all frantic searching for an additional guest and at the same time trying to get one of us to go home. But he was serious: he took some of the common superstitions in deadly earnest.

Another instance—a literary one—of his seriousness comes to my mind. In a recent book, *Joyce and Shakespeare*, the writer says, "One can almost hear Joyce chuckle as he casually tossed out a hint that Victor Bérard's *The Phoenicians and the Odyssey* might be interesting to investigate." But Joyce neither chuckled nor was casual when he talked about Bérard; he was deeply impressed—as my husband has already mentioned—by this scholar's revelations as to the origin of the *Odyssey*, and when Bérard died he made a point of attending his funeral, and thought of his death as a great loss. Indeed, when Joyce wanted to pay an intimate friend an unusual compliment he presented him or her with a copy of Bérard's translation of the *Odyssey*: I have such a presentation copy at my elbow.

In some ways Joyce could be very difficult and even intolerable. He was angry with me because I made friends with some French people who were Thomists in a different way from himself, who was "steeled in the school of old Aquinas." And he was both cross and amused, later, when I attended the lectures of Pierre Janet, the greatest of the French psychologists, and went to the Asylum of Saint Anne on Sunday mornings to the sessions of the psychologist Georges Dumas. "You could learn as much psychology from yourself as from these fellows," he said to me.

Joyce spoke with this dislike of the well-known official psychologists, but it did not take much penetration to perceive how much he had been affected by them. He himself was a man of rather simple psychology, with simple reactions, but with a very complex mind and imagination, and with a leaning toward odd learning which I think of as Irish.

Joyce's intellectual training had begun early, and he had won prizes in the Intermediate examinations (though in Paris he was cynical about such competitions). His erudition was partly a product of the monstrous grind that marked the scholastic career of a youthful, Jesuit-trained Dubliner of that period. But the basis of his learning was chiefly the education we had both received at the Royal University in Dublin. Though some years apart in age, we had studied the same languages, the same grammars and texts in these languages, and had the same university degree: in modern languages and literature.

However, what I had retained of that education was as nothing to what Joyce had kept; and the kinds of knowledge each of us had retained were very different. I had only the slightest interest in the beginnings of modern languages, in the development of linguistics, in grammar in the early periods of language development. To all these philological questions Joyce applied himself with intensity of interest: he knew by heart paragraphs or pages of early Anglo-Saxon, of Italian of before Dante's time, of pre-Luther German, and the *Serment de Strasbourg*. At parties he delighted in repeating with me the rhymes we had both learned out of grammars, doggerel meant to help one remember rules, declensions, and genders. Why saying over such lines as:

> Common are to either sex
> *Artifex* and *opifex*,
> *Conviva, vates, advena,*
> *Testis, civis, incola.*

gave him such hilarious pleasure I never could understand. He would cry:

> "With *nemo* never let me see
> *Neminis* or *nemine*,"

and then double over with laughter. "Oh, the imperiousness of it! 'Never let me see!'"

## IV.  PADRAIC COLUM

One day when I went into the Shakespeare Head, Miss
Beach said, "Mr. Joyce wants to know when he can see you."
Her emphasis implied a singling out—the "you" was particular.
She remarked that the *Anna Livia Plurabelle* episode from
Joyce's new work was to be published as a booklet, and she
was happy to think that part of the new work was going to a
wider public. Mr. Joyce thought it should have an introduc-
tion. Did I know anyone who could do it? Miss Beach asked.
I told her I would think it over and offer a few possibilities to
Joyce when I saw him.

He suggested, when we met, that we should take a walk
together. I remember as we went along I read an advertise-
ment that was across a street. "Can you really read what is
over there?" Joyce asked me in surprise. Then I realized how
poor his eyesight was. His eyes often now had the lonely, patient look of the blind.

On and off we talked of who might possibly do the introduction, and we always came back to the fact that the person
who did it would, as well as being interested in this later work
of his, have to know Dublin. But it was hard to fix on anyone
who would sponsor *Anna Livia* on her going forth. Then he
told me how he had got the French printer to cut short delays
and bring out *Ulysses* in a reasonable time. "I wrote to him
that my fortieth birthday was on February second of that year,
and that it would be of great consequence to me to have my
book out by then. He got it out for me, as I knew a French
printer would." Knowing Joyce's indirection, I got the point
of the story. "Would you like me to do the introduction,
Joyce?" "You're the man I have in mind." And on that we
turned back.

Miss Beach was all smiles when I told her I was the person
selected. She had known where the choice lay when she discussed the matter with me. And so I read the episode that

I had first heard when Joyce read it to my wife and myself, on our earlier visit, with another interest. "What is the name of the river by your birthplace?" Joyce had asked me after that first reading. "I'll put it in," he said when I told him. And there, in the catalogue of the great and famous rivers, was the very local Camlin.

My wife and I had dinner with Joyce and Nora the evening before we left Paris. I read him the introduction. "I like it immensely," he said, and I shall always remember how appreciative he made the words. As it came out of my association with Joyce in the days when *Work in Progress* was pristine, I set down a part of the introduction[1] here:

Anna Livia Plurabelle *is concerned with the flowing of a River. There have gone into it the things that make a people's inheritance: landscape, myth, and history; there have gone into it, too, what is characteristic of a people: jests and fables. It is epical in its largeness of meaning and its multiplicity of interest.* . . .

. . . *"O tell me all about Anna Livia! I want to hear all about Anna Livia. Well, you know Anna Livia? Yes, of course, we all know Anna Livia. Tell me all. Tell me now."* So [the episode] *begins, and at once we are in the water as it bubbles and hurries at its source. The first passage gives us the sight of the River, the second gives us the River as it is seen and heard and felt. The whole of the episode gives us something besides the sight and sound and feeling of water.* . . . *There are moments in our lifetime when, even though inarticulate, we are all poets, moments that are probably very frequent in childhood, moments when a bird hopping on the grass or a bush in blossom is something we could look upon for hours with a mind constantly stirred and forming images and thoughts that range through the visible world, through history, and through the experiences of one's own lifetime. Such moments might come to us in any place. They would come most appropriately whilst watching the flow of water. It is this range we get in this episode: over and above the sight and sound and feeling of water there is in* Anna Livia Plura-

[1] Published in the signed, limited edition of *Anna Livia Plurabelle*, brought out by Crosby Gaige in New York in 1928.

belle *that range of images and thoughts, those free combinations of words and ideas, that might arise in us, if with a mind inordinately full and on a day singularly happy we watched a river and thought upon a river and traveled along a river from its source to its mouth.*

But in this episode the mind's range has a boundary: the range is never beyond the river banks nor away from the city toward which the river is making its slow-moving, sometimes hurrying way. Dublin, the city once seventh in Christendom, Dublin that was founded by sea-rovers, Dublin with its worthies, its sojourners, its odd characters, not as they are known to the readers of history books, but as they live in the minds of some dwellers by the Liffey, is in this episode; Dublin, the Ford of Hurdles, the entrance into the plain of Ireland, the city so easily taken, so uneasily held. And the River itself, less in magnitude than the tributary of a tributary of one of the important rivers, becomes enlarged until it includes hundreds of the world's rivers. How many have their names woven into the tale of Anna Livia Plurabelle? More than five hundred, I believe. "She thought she's sankh neathe the ground with nymphant shame when he gave her the tigris eye." In that sentence three of the world's great rivers are mentioned. . . . How beautifully the sentence that goes before it gives the flow of water! "She sid herself she hardly know whuon the annals her graveller was, a dynast of Leinster, a wolf of the sea, or what he did or how blyth she played or how, when, why, where and who offon he jumpnad her and how it was gave her away. She was just a young thin pale soft shy slim slip of a thing then, sauntering, by Silvamoonlake and he was a heavy trudging lurching lieabroad of a Curraghman, making his hay for whose sun to shine on, as tough as the oaktrees (peats be with them!) used to rustle that time down by the dykes of killing Kildare, that forstfellfoss with a plash across her."

There will be many interpretations of Anna Livia Plurabelle—as many as the ideas that might come to one who watched the flowing of the actual river. . . . To myself there comes the recollection of a feeling I had when, as a child, the first time in Dublin I crossed a bridge with an elder of mine beside me. I imagine other children's minds would have been *occupied with such thoughts as occupied mine then. The city—who named it? The pavements—who laid them down? The statues—what had the men done that they should claim that men should look upon them now and that men should have looked upon them in one's father's and one's father's father's time? The River—who named it? Why that name and no other? And from what place did the River come? The mystery of beginnings filled the mind. And, combining with the questions that came, there were things that had to be noted—the elder one walked beside, now, strangely enough, become a man of the city, knowing its lore, being saluted by its inhabitants, the apple one bought and ate and the penny one paid for it, the beggar woman on the bridge with her blinded eyes and her doleful voice. . . . I feel in this tale of Anna Livia Plurabelle the mystery of beginnings as it is felt through, as it combines with, a hundred stray, significant, trifling things. . . .*

*Its author, the most daring of innovators, has decided to be as local as a hedge-poet. James Joyce writes as if it might be taken for granted that his readers know, not only the city he writes about, but its little shops and its little shows, the nicknames that have been given to its near-great, the cant phrases that have been used on its side streets. "The ghost-white horse of the Peppers," he writes, and some of us remember that there was an act in a circus called "Pepper's Ghost," and that there is an Irish play called* The White Horse of the Peppers—*a play in which ancestral acres are recovered through the speed of a horse. Through these memories a mythical shape appears on the banks of the River. This local-ness belongs to James Joyce's innovations: all his innovations are toward giving us what he writes about in its own atmos-phere and with its own proper motion. And only those things which have been encountered day after day in some definite place can be given with their own atmosphere, their own motion. . . .*

*Anna Livia Plurabelle—two washerwomen tell her story. As it begins, the evening sun, we fancy, is dabbling the water; as it closes, night is closing in. Voices become remote. Meta-morphoses come upon all that has been looked upon and talked about. The women, when we look to see them again,*

*have been changed, one into a stone, and the other into an*
*elm tree. It is any story that might have been babbled about*
*anywhere . . . a tale told of Shaun and Shem. . . .*


## V.  PADRAIC COLUM


*Time and Western Man*, by Wyndham Lewis, was published between one of our visits to Paris and the next, and
there was something in it about Joyce.

In the days before *Ulysses* and *Remembrance of Things*
*Past* had set up new landmarks, Ezra Pound, James Joyce, and
Wyndham Lewis—a trio at the time in Paris—represented the
dynamism of a new generation; Lewis' *Tarr* was ranked by
Pound with *Portrait of the Artist*. Now, along with Charlie
Chaplin and the author of *Gentlemen Prefer Blondes*, Lewis
listed Joyce as a nibbler at Western man's concept of time.
I don't know if Joyce minded this. But there was in the book,
as well as an abstract consideration of his work, a projection
of Joyce as a person: out of *Portrait of the Artist* Lewis had
drawn a background for him that was detracting in the con-
text given. True, in that novel Joyce had depicted a family life
that was seedy and sordid. But that life was an accidental cir-
cumstance, in Joyce's mind; innately he was, as was his father,
an Irish gentleman, and to take the background of Stephen
Dedalus as literally his own was to take from his personal
dignity.

The thesis of *Time and Western Man* interested me, and
at one of our meetings I talked to Joyce about the book. I remarked that Wyndham Lewis seemed to be approaching the
position of the Catholic Church. "You have taken the words
out of my mouth!" Joyce exclaimed. "He is preparing to make
a clamorous conversion." (Here it should be said that this did
not turn out to be the case.)

Wyndham Lewis, Joyce went on to say, had come in handily
when he was composing the episode of *Work in Progress* that
was now out in *transition*, a version of the fable of the Ant

and the Grasshopper—in Joycean, the Ondt and the Grace-hoper. He had wanted certain features for the ungracious and purposeful Ondt, and Lewis had provided them. It seemed Joyce had had a grievance against him before *Time and Western Man* came out, for the author of *Tarr* had said, years before, to the author of *Dubliners* and *Portrait of the Artist*, "You should go to South America." Joyce took it that Lewis wanted to get him off the European scene. And to get him to give up writing—for if one didn't write in Spanish, why go to South America to write? Remembrance of this intended dismissal by Lewis gave particular animation, Joyce thought, to his portrait of the well-fixed Ondt:

*The Ondt was a weltall fellow, raumybult and abelboodied, bynear saw altitudinous wee a schelling in kopfers. He was sair sair sullemn and chairmanlooking when he was not making spaces in his psyche, but, laus! when he wore making spaces on his ikey, he ware mouche mothst secred and muravyingly wisechairmanlooking.*

And one can find a Picasso-like image in this.

Reading the episode over after that, I came to a verse whose rhythm was familiar. Where had I come across it before?

*I forgive you, grondt Ondt, said the Gracehoper, weeping,*
*For their sukes of the sakes you are safe in whose keeping.*
*Teach Floh and Luse polkas, show Bienie where's sweet*
*And be sure Vespatilla finds fat ones to heat.*
*As I once played the piper I must now pay the count*
*So saida to Moyhammlet and marhaba to your Mount!*

Wasn't it the same as:

*Here lies David Garrick, describe me, who can,*
*An abridgement of all that was pleasant in man;*
. . . . . . . . . . . . . . . . . . . . . . . . .
*On the stage he was natural, simple, affecting;*
*'Twas only that when he was off he was acting.*

The poet was Goldsmith and the poem was "Retaliation." So Joyce had written the verse and the episode in which the verse occurs as a retaliation.

That the author of *The Vicar of Wakefield* and *The De-
serted Village* meant so much to the writer of *Ulysses* and
*Chamber Music* was something of a discovery.[1] And it was no
misapprehension, for when I mentioned it to Joyce, at dinner
not long after that, I learned that he had a warm regard for
that excellent man of letters, Oliver Goldsmith. He became
genial when he spoke of him, and quoted with enjoyment from
"Retaliation" the lines about Burke:

> *Though fraught with all learning, yet straining his throat*
> *To persuade Tommy Townshend to lend him a vote.*

He was unassuming, Joyce went on to say, praising Goldsmith for personal qualities. He spoke of it as virtue in a man
to make no disturbance about what he does or the life he has
to live. But was Joyce himself always unassuming? I remembered:

---

[1] I made a further discovery some time after writing this, one that
shows Joyce's fondness for Goldsmith goes back to his schooldays. As I
was reading the manuscript of this memoir in the Arts Club, Dublin,
a member, Mr. George O'Donnell, spoke to me about a book he had
had since his schooldays at Belvedere College, where he was a classmate of Joyce, on the front page of which Joyce had written a piece
about him. He very kindly offered to lend me the book, and I have it
before me now. It is *A Concise History of Ireland*, by P. W. Joyce,
published in 1894. The class in Belvedere had been reading Goldsmith's "Retaliation," and the sixteen-year-old Joyce singled out one
of his classmates for an address that echoes Goldsmith's mock
epitaphs. I believe it is the earliest piece of Joyce's verse that has been
found:

G. O'DONNELL

> *Poor little Georgie, the son of a lackey,*
> *Famous for 'murphies,' spirits, and 'baccy,*
> *Renowned all around for a feathery head*
> *Which had a tendency to become red.*
> *His genius was such that all men used to stare,*
> *His appearance was that of a bull at a fair.*
> *The pride of Kilmainham, the joy of the class,*
> *A moony, a loony, an idiot, an ass.*
> *Drumcondra's production, and by the same rule,*
> *The prince of all pot-boys, a regular fool.*
> *All hail to the beauteous, the lovely, all hail*
> *And hail to his residence in Portland gaol.*

*Where they have crouched and crawled and prayed*
*I stand, the self-doomed, unafraid,*
*Unfellowed, friendless and alone,*
*Indifferent as the herring-bone,*
*Firm as the mountain-ridges where*
*I flash my antlers on the air.*

Joyce, perhaps, had reacted youthfully to a hurt given him in youthful days. Had he become mellow now? More likely the essential Joyce was the one who, in that youthful essay on Mangan, had asked: "What is so courteous and so patient as a great faith?"

At that same dinner a writer from whom Joyce was supposed to have inherited something—Jonathan Swift—was mentioned. As a Dublin man, if nothing more, Joyce might be expected to offer tribute to Swift. But all he said of him was, "He made a mess of two women's lives." When I remarked on Swift's intensity, Joyce said with quiet conviction, "There is more intensity in a single passage of Mangan's than in all Swift's writing."[2] (We were all Irish at the table, and so the literary figures discussed were mainly Irish.) Though I could not agree with his estimate of Mangan—for Joyce it was highly extravagant—I was delighted that even now that he was a writer with a European reputation he had kept his youthful admiration for a poet who is hardly known outside Ireland.

Joyce read very little at the time, due to the poor state of his eyes, and so I was surprised to find the conversation at

[2] I wonder would Joyce have been interested in Swift's linguistic deviations? The Dean and Thomas Sheridan wrote to each other in a mixture of English and Latin; these letters as published by Dr. George Mayhew in the *Bulletin* of the John Rylands Library, Manchester, have the look of passages from *Finnegans Wake*. Both Swift and Sheridan took trouble with these compositions; both made preliminary drafts. Here is Swift's letter to Sheridan joshing him for an alleged attempt to separate himself from the old Irish stock: "*Cum cum surdo notu prae tendit I do advisu, uras mere Iris has feli mone alas tego Sui ne ora nodo Horti ore venas Machina Maro: Praes heri dando ad MACto ure na morO, ure offas sol da pede agri as ani in Monster Orco nautis.*" Which being interpreted reads: "Come come sir do not pretend it I do advise you, you're as mere Irish as Phelim O'Neill, as Teague O'Swiney or an O'Dogherty or even as MacNamara: Pray Sheridan do add Mac to your name or O, you're of as old a pedigree as any in Munster or Connaught is."

that dinner keeping to its literary turn. He spoke of Henry James, remarking that it was evident that he had influenced Proust. He praised *Portrait of a Lady*, dwelling with much delight on the presentation of Isabel Archer. *Madame Bovary* he said he had read recently but had found the narrative part tedious.

The talk went back to Irish writers. For Yeats' poetry Joyce had—but this was no news—a high regard; he mentioned that he had collaborated on a translation into Italian of *The Countess Cathleen*. Of course I remembered that a lyric from this play, "Who will go drive with Fergus now?" had possessed the mind of Stephen Dedalus at a sorrowful time of his life.

Having spoken of Yeats, Joyce went on to speak of Synge and George Moore. He had also helped to translate Synge's *Riders to the Sea* into Italian. He said he thought the play too short to have a tragic scope. I disagreed with him in this, saying that in the stage production the keening of the women who come into the house gives it another dimension.

George Moore had given Joyce one of his recent books; he was sorry it was not *Esther Waters*, which was the novel of Moore he admired. Other names came up as the company talked, Arthur Symons' among them. Symons' translations of Verlaine, Joyce took it on himself to say, were equal to the originals.

As always, it was pleasant to talk with Joyce in an after-dinner mood. There was nothing pretentious or solemn in what he said, but one knew he had enjoyed the books he spoke of, that they remained in his mind as a deposit of experience, and that he honored their writers as men who had done their work and done it well. And now, becoming accustomed to his indirection, I could not help thinking that in speaking of certain writers he wanted to reveal his fundamental—as against his reported—opinion of them. Yeats: had he really said to him, "We have met too late; you are too old to be influenced by me"? Yet his fundamental opinion was shown by the fact that he had helped to translate *The Countess Cathleen*. Had he really laughed when Arthur Symons mentioned Balzac? Maybe. But who better than Symons could make verse that was colloquial and musical at the same time? George Moore? Certainly Joyce had had a dig at him:

> *Written by Moore, a genuine gent*
> *That lives on his property's ten per cent.*

But Moore's privilege did not obscure the fact that he had written a first-rate novel, in *Esther Waters*.

He had mentioned *Remembrance of Things Past*. With the way his eyes were, Joyce could not have gone through the whole work. But he had met Proust. A certain hostess had thought she could create a historic occasion by bringing the two celebrated authors together in her salon, and Joyce told us about the event. He had arrived about ten o'clock. Eleven o'clock came and no Proust. Twelve o'clock came and still no Proust. At 1:00 A.M. Proust entered the salon, dressed, Joyce said, "like the hero of *The Sorrows of Satan*." The two authors were presented to each other, and the company arranged itself so as not to miss anything of the conversation. Here is what was said:

*Proust:* Ah, Monsieur Joyce . . . You know the Princess . . .
*Joyce:* No, Monsieur.
*Proust:* Ah. You know the Countess . . .
*Joyce:* No, Monsieur.
*Proust:* Then you know Madame . . .
*Joyce:* No, Monsieur.

And that terminated the Proust-Joyce meeting of minds. It was probably characteristic of Proust. It was also characteristic of Joyce: he was wont to be taciturn in the presence of the featured great.

## VI. PADRAIC COLUM

Around 1929 I had an opportunity of helping Joyce at his writing table. True, the help was slight, and there were others in his entourage who also lent a hand and a head. But my helping him meant an association with Joyce the writer, meant a meeting of his mind and mine on the problems of writing as he saw them, and this temporary association en-

ables me to write of the reflective and productive side of
Joyce.

The Joyces were living in Square Robiac then, and it was
a relatively carefree time for all of them, it now seems to me,
looking back on it. For Joyce a further operation on his eyes,
that anguish that he had to face periodically, was not immi-
nent. The affairs of Lucia and Giorgio were under control.
Nora was serene. Outside troubles had not yet begun to make
themselves felt.

I remember an incident that seems to me to give the tone
of this carefree season. I had come to the Joyce apartment for
dinner, a clear evening with the assiduous author having been
indicated. The rest of the family had gone out; Joyce was there
alone, with Herbert Gorman.

I was greeted with a certain boisterousness. "We've just
worked your name into *Work in Progress*," Gorman announced. I made a suitable reply. (The name is in the book,
but, I am forced to think, impersonally: "—The S.S. Paudraic's
in the harbour.") We sat down to dinner, served by the maid.
All through the meal Joyce and Gorman made remarks, the
point of which I didn't get, although it was obvious they had
an amusemer t value for my table companions. When we had
finished dinner one said to the other, "Don't you think he
ought to know?" I realized there was a joke, that the joke was
on me—but what was it? The two comedians, Joyce and Gorman, stood there, one sparking the other. Then I was told
what the joke was: Friday, and I had eaten meat! But I was
far from being covered with confusion; the abstinence Joyce
credited me with was mythical.

In the course of the evening Joyce said to me, "If your
grandfather or mine came into this apartment we would be
shocked." He was not speaking of them as ghostly visitants:
he meant that their costume, their appearance as molded by
the period, the mental and moral prepossessions of two gen-
erations ago, would be not only surprising but uncanny. It is
easy to say that even in the case of a grandfather of whom
one has only a childish recollection there would be a good
deal to mitigate the shock of confrontation; from photographs
we would know the appearance and the garb, from letters,
the manner of expression. Yes, Joyce agreed, when I offered

this, but think of the oddness of the appearance of Mr. Gladstone or President Lincoln! But wouldn't the mental proc-
esses of these personages prevent any alienation? They would,
Joyce conceded, if they delivered them to us as recorded for
us. But think of getting the whole of either of them in a modern apartment—Gladstone's noble sentences with Gladstone's
pomposity, Lincoln's memorable phrases with Lincoln's jokes!
No doubt the confrontation with visitants from two gener-
ations back would give us the shock that Joyce announced.
And I suppose this means that when Joyce in *Finnegans Wake*
treats of characters in the past—they are all in the past—he
has to make them odd, terrifically odd. He has to treat them
as a caricaturist would.

Here and now I take from the shelf a book boxed in green:
*Haveth Childers Everywhere*, by James Joyce. In *Finnegans
Wake* what is in this small volume[1] begins on page 532 with
"—Amtsadam, sir, to you! Eternest cittas, heil!" In a language
nearly as special as Joyce's own, the printers of the volume
tell us that it has been "composed by hand in freshly cast
Elzévir Corps 16 . . . on imperial hand-made iridescent Ja-
pan." The format is expressive of the author—the parchment
cover, the green lettering of the title, the long, well-spaced
page. And I expect that in Joyce's mind this format corre-
sponded with the episode related. The book is dated 1930.

This is the volume that certain members of the clan, myself
included, helped Joyce to get out—working, as far as I remember, from what had been published in *transition*. One of the
things we conferred about on the evening when my abstinence
was broken down was the proper person to write an introduction to the fragment (actually *Haveth Childers Everywhere*
was published without an introduction). There was no question of my introducing this fragment, as I had done a previous
one, nor of James Stephens, nor any other literary man, doing
it. This introduction was a job for an architect or a mayor or
a building contractor, as the episode dealt with the building
of the city. It was curious, but it was also characteristic of
Joyce that he thought anybody so externally minded as a
builder or an administrator would be competent to write an

1 A limited de luxe edition published in Paris by Babou and Kahane.

introduction to the piece. He actually believed that, on one level anyway, his later work had a public appeal. "My brandold Dublin lindub, the free, the froh, the frothy freshener"—that really is a good slogan for the Dublin brew, Guinness', and Joyce was actually disappointed that the Guinnesses did not use it instead of the commonplace "Guinness is good for you." But maybe they will appropriate it some time—"the free, the froh, the frothy freshener." "Lindub," Dublin scrambled, is the Irish for black ale.

As I look over the text of *Haveth Childers Everywhere*, I come on "tendulcis tunes like water parted fluted up from the westinders while from gorges in the east came the strife of ourangoontangues." "Water parted," I cried as I typed this passage. "You're drawing on Goldsmith, Joyce." I remembered that "Water Parted" and "The Minute in Ariadne" were the genteel tunes that Tony Lumpkin's servants affected. Joyce laughed, as one whose virtuosity has been recognized—the laugh of the man who has brought something home that the family didn't think he could get. Goldsmith, the Dublin student, who played on the flute—how gently and charmingly he comes into the city that H.C.E. is engaged in founding. Joyce hummed over "Water parted from the say."

Here Comes Everybody, who is the Finnegan of the Wake, gives his initials, H.C.E., to the title of this fragment. The builder of the city, he speaks for himself. And, as Nimrod and Romulus accomplished their tasks, so he accomplishes his under the shadow of a crime. He has first, in the episode, to defend himself. The charge brought against him is vague and shifting. It has to do with those "gretched youngsters" whom he encountered in a park or garden—locally, the Phoenix Park. The speaker is embarrassed and stutters in the opening of his defense: "I am bubub brought up under a camel act of dynasties long out of print." He speaks for himself in justification and pride; his creation is the city, the city standing against the flowing river of *Anna Livia Plurabelle*.

And as Joyce introduced the names of the world's rivers into the river-fragment published earlier, so into this one he introduces the names of the world's cities. The salutation in the opening recalls two cities: "Amtsadam" and "Eternest cittas." Sometimes these references seem merely "cute," as "ye

litel chuch rond ye coner" which, making littler "The Little
Church Around the Corner," recalls New York. H.C.E.'s is a
long oration, interrupted by radio announcements. For all its
incomprehensibility, as regards language, it projects a character—the city boss, the party leader, shrewd in defense, prideful
in his achievement. Its pattern is the Irish Speech from the
Dock. It ends with a great declamation.

What did my contribution to this production amount to?
I typed pages. From time to time I was asked to suggest a word
that would be more obscure than the word already there.
Joyce would consider my offer, his eyes, their pupils enlarged
behind glasses, expectant, his face intent, his figure upstand-
ing. "I can't use it," was what he would say five times out of
six. Two contributions of mine are in the text, and they got
in by accident. One is in the passage about the Lying-in Hospital: in the text it is "the bethel of Solyman's" because of
Bethel Solomons who was head of the Rotunda at one time—
I think Joyce knew him ("I accouched their rotundaties").
"What's the Irish for mother?" Joyce asked me. "*Mauher*. But
you ought to know, Joyce, because John McCormack sings
something with *maureen machree* in it." "I'll use that." And
so we have "the maugher machrees and the auntieparthe-
nopes." With the distorted Greek and the distorted Gaelic
words alongside each other he brings distant peoples together.
At the very end of the declamation another contribution of
mine, also of accidental adoption, appears. Having made the
roads, H.C.E. is describing all the vehicles on them. "The car-
riage driven by one person seated on a high box behind—what
is it called?" Joyce asked. I didn't know, but I said the fellow
usually looked very "lawdy-daw." "I'll put that in." And there
it is, at the very end—"My damsells softsidesaddled, covertly,
covertly, and Lawdy Dawe a perch behind."
Joyce was one of the great masters of language, and he could
be that only through a love of words, a response to shades of
their meaning, a knowledge of their history. Besides that, he
had private associations with words, associations that could,
apparently, evoke an episode in his life—those that he spoke
of were comic.
I see him now standing in the middle of his apartment,

laughing reminiscently because of a word that has come up.
"The caca cad!" H.C.E. cries, denouncing an accuser. "A cad
on a bicycle" had asked Joyce's father for a match in the
Phoenix Park. Relating the incident when he got home, his
father had used the word "cad" abusively. But what did "cad"
mean? A cadet, a younger son. And why should "younger son"
amount to a term of abuse? "A cad on a bicycle"—Joyce was
in a convulsion of laughter as he repeated it. Was the comedy
in the fact that his father should be enraged because a young
man on a bicycle addressed him? Or was it that the dark ex-
panse of garden, a man asking for a light, the ferocious reaction of the one accosted, suggested the comic side of a
myth? Or was it the passage of "cadet" into "cad" that was
comic?

I have suggested that in *Finnegans Wake* Joyce's art is akin
to the caricaturist's. It presents the human being as an oddity.
But its real intention is to be wittily revealing by exaggerating
some feature or some tendency. In this connection there comes
into my mind the cartoon of the German army marching into
the Balkans along the great nose of Ferdinand of Bulgaria.
The revelation that was in this caricature depended on the
public knowledge of the outsized royal nose. In *Finnegans
Wake* a public knowledge of this kind is not available. For
instance: there was a character prominent in Norse Dublin
named Kettil Flatnose (I expect all that is known about him
is his name), and there was a contemporary of Joyce's—an ac-
quaintance, perhaps—named Laurence Kettle, who was in
charge of the powerhouse that gave electricity to the city and
the lighthouses. And so we have "my duindleeng lunas, help-
helped of Kettil Flashnose . . . through all Livania's volted
ampire, from anodes to cathodes and from the topazolites of
Mourne, Wykinloeflare, by Arklow's sapphire siomen's lure
and Wexterford's hook and crook lights to the polders of Hy
Kinsella." And there are other figures in this particular episode whose circumstances are even less public than those of
the personages mentioned here.

For the writing of *Finnegans Wake* Joyce had to have much
information. The state of his eyes prevented continuous reading. Now anyone who has read *Portrait of the Artist* or *Ulysses* knows that Joyce had read immensely; he had a retentive

memory besides. However, as he was entering new areas now he had to have new prototypes, and these had to be supplied with idioms and idiosyncrasies. This meant a mass of reading, and the reading had to be farmed out among his friends. What they were to read for could not be defined. He did not want any of us to brief him, for example, on astronomy or finance. But the name of a star or a term in finance—"sterling," say—would give him something that he needed.

I have mentioned earlier that Joyce once asked me to read *Hudibras* for him. Evidently this reading was planned, for he had the books ready—two old-fashioned volumes, I remember. He did not want me to give him incidents or quotations from Butler's poem; for him its interest was in the fact that, like *Don Quixote*, it had two associated and contrasting characters. How was the association and the contrast made? As we went for walks along the streets I would tell him about the doings of the pair. What use he made of the information I never found out.

And because *Finnegans Wake* dealt with night life he wanted to know about other books that proceeded from night life. One was *The Arabian Nights*. Of course he knew that practically all the stories in the collection so named are as much of the daylight as of the night. Still, the framework has to do with nights, and, we are told, the art of the collection originated in "night-walkers' stories." Joyce wanted *The Arabian Nights* read by someone who would tell him some of its features, so he sent over to my apartment a sixteen-volume set of Burton's translation. The first thing I reported interested him: back of the Arabian stories were Persian stories: in fact, the names of the storyteller and her sister were Persian. The fact of one culture leading into another was always fascinating to Joyce, and he wanted to know if there was a parallel between the Persian stories giving rise to the Arabian and the Celtic stories giving rise to the stories of the Arthurian cycle. And what did the names of the storyteller and her sister mean? I read the sixteen volumes with great delight, naturally (I had read only Lane's four volumes previously), and talked to Joyce about various features in them. The Caliph walking about at night with his Vizier must appear on some page of

*Finnegans Wake,* but the only lines I am sure derived from my reading are those about the "night-talking sisters."


## VII.   MARY M. COLUM


The grand duchess of Dublin, Sarah Purser, was over in Paris about that time. She had not been there for several years, and she wrote to ask me to get a hotel for her. We were staying in a small one in the rue Montparnasse and we arranged rooms for her there. She had been an art student in Paris when Julien's atelier was the whole world of the European art student, and she had put in a lifetime of fine painting since. Rich and of a very distinguished family, she had dominated Dublin by her wit for fifty years.

She wanted to meet James Joyce, and as I knew that Joyce was always willing to meet Dublin people and probably had some extra interest in Sarah, I sent him and Nora an invitation to the dinner I was giving for her. Whom else should I ask? James and Cynthia Stephens were staying in Paris at the time, and I decided to ask them to come. James Stephens and James Joyce, the two who had celebrated Dublin life in such different ways, had never met—in fact, they had shied away from meeting each other.

The proprietor of our hotel, a Swiss, had a restaurant next door to the hotel; being told the name of one of our guests, he put up an exquisite dinner for us in a private room. James Stephens could not be with us, as he had to go to London that evening; Cynthia came, however, and I put her beside Joyce. There were soon talking at the rate of a hunt. Cynthia, not for a moment awed by his reputation, and talking in a voice that echoed Dublin, won Joyce completely over. He was courteous, of course, to the witty lady who stood for all that was academic and social in the Irish capital, but it was plain that it was the wife of a fellow writer who had made the great impression on him.

Cynthia Stephens invited Joyce to their apartment. How he

with his nearly blind eyes managed to struggle up four flights of stairs to their little flat was a mystery to me, but he did, and did it carrying six bottles of Swiss wine as a present for the Stephenses.

Joyce and James Stephens, having waited so long to meet, became fast friends. Joyce discovered important "correspondences" between himself and Stephens, in this case based partly on fact: the two men did have the same birthday—February 2 —and had been born (they said) in the same year. Stephens' first name was the same as Joyce's, and his second name, except for the final "s," the same as that of the hero of *Portrait of the Artist* and *Ulysses*. And both had two children, a boy and a girl each. With all this in common, how could they have helped being friends?

## PADRAIC COLUM

Joyce and James Stephens were a great deal together after that: we found this companionship a happy feature of the Joyce establishment during our sojourns in Paris. The author of *Ulysses* had come under the spell of the author of *The Crock of Gold*. And who wouldn't? No one in the world had so much spontaneity with so much gusto as James Stephens, so much wisdom with so much nonsense, so much fantasy with so much poetry. Why not speak of his humor? Because Stephen's humor was not detachable: it was the rainbow above the waterfall of his exuberant discourse. Joyce would often repeat with delight a saying of Stephens' that had some strange flash in it.

Like Joyce, Stephens had come out of a Dublin that had a musical tradition, and, without Joyce's style, he would sing Dublin street songs. His eyes closed and his hands clasped before him, his figure slight and stooping, he would regale us with:

*She wheeled a wheelbarrow through streets wide and narrow,*
*Crying "Cockles and mussels, alive, alive O!"*

and then:

*She died of a fayver, and nothing could save her,*
*And that was the end of sweet Molly Malone.*

Before going on to the last verse he would make a comment: "We are an unbeatable people, and death isn't the end for us, as it might be for other people." And so, with renewed energy:

*But her ghost wheels a barrow through streets wide and narrow,*
*Crying "Cockles and mussels, alive, alive O!"*

If he had not been a poet and storyteller, James Stephens would have been a clown in the great style. I would see Joyce looking at him, as Stephens, with his brown eyes and his mobile face, was singing something about "Mick Mulligan's terrier dog," and would guess a relationship between them that was different from the occult one that Joyce had announced, based on dates and names they had in common. They had an occupational relationship: they were both of the company of a group of strolling players. I could see them in a booth or on a stage in the open air, one appearing and singing some great aria, then the other coming on with a monologue composed of poetry and fantasy. What a performance that pair could give!

Joyce's attachment to Stephens was shown by a retort that came from him when I questioned something that Stephens had done. He and Cynthia had left Paris to be house guests of Lady Londonderry. "Isn't it a wonder," I said to Joyce, "that James Stephens would have anything to do with a descendant of Castlereagh?" Joyce did not answer for a moment; then he said with some rancor, "Haven't I seen you talking with John Dillon's son?"

I will have to explain to the non-Irish reader why the retort was a staggering surprise to me. Lord Londonderry was a descendant of the Castlereagh who, in the most cynical fashion, destroyed the Irish Legislature. John Dillon belonged to the group in Parnell's party that deposed him as leader. In Joyce's time and mine John Dillon, backed by an Irish constituency, worked for the restoration of the Legislature. That Joyce should put John Dillon and Castlereagh in the same class— even out of friendship for Stephens—was inexplicable to me. John Dillon's son was in Paris: he was a philologist studying Sanskrit and the connections of Old Irish with it. My wife and I had brought this young man, Myles Dillon, to Joyce's, and

Joyce had treated him with his usual courtesy. And all the time he was remembering that he was entertaining the son of a man who had helped to bring about the downfall of the Uncrowned King!

Pondering on this, I found something magnificent in the unreason of Joyce's loyalty to an individual who had stirred his imagination. What passion a boy of ten or eleven must have known as he watched Parnell's downfall! Was it this that separated him from all political interests? "Colum, this is the second time I have come into the room and found you talking politics," he once admonished me.

## MARY M. COLUM

Up to nearly the end of his life Joyce was waiting patiently, I think, for a signal from the Irish government, inviting him back to place bay leaves in his hair. However, the Irish political people are peculiarly indifferent to what their great writers have done for the country. The invitation never came Joyce's way.

He rejoiced, however, in any sign of Dublin's interest in him. Of course he knew that he was admired and read, by this time, in Dublin; but any overt sign of that fact made him happy. Once when my husband and I were in a café in Montmartre a Dubliner who recognized Padraic came up and spoke to us. This man was in Paris to attend a football match between an Irish and a French team. We soon found that he was soaked in *Ulysses*, but without a suspicion of cliquishness: for him the episodes were transcriptions of the life he knew. As he talked about Mr. Bloom's day my husband and I agreed that here was the very man Joyce would like to talk to. I telephoned to ask if I might bring him round, and Joyce answered enthusiastically, "Bring him right now."

The Dublin citizen was dazzled at being presented to the author of *Ulysses*. It was Sunday, and the family had gone somewhere; Joyce was alone in the apartment, clad in a dressing gown.

As soon as the visitor, whose name was Pugh, began to talk Joyce became gleeful. Mr. Pugh had a family history that ap-

pealed to the writer of *Work in Progress*. He was from a family
of glassmakers. In the eighteenth century when, to finish off
Irish competition, the English glassmakers had a law passed
that prevented existing firms from taking apprentices, some
glassmakers in Dublin took to desperate expedients. They had
young glassmakers kidnaped in England and conveyed, somehow or other, to Dublin. Mr. Pugh's forefather had come over
to Ireland in this remarkable way. It was just the sort of story
to catch Joyce's attention, and I expect some researcher will
find something about Mr. Pugh's forefather in *Finnegans
Wake*.

Joyce and his visitor soon got talking of haunts they had
frequented in Dublin. "What sort of person really knows Dublin?" my husband asked. Mr. Pugh answered categorically:
"The man that knocks about." The creator of Mr. Bloom was
sure he was right.

After a while Joyce handed the Dubliner a copy of *Ulysses*.
Selecting the barroom episode, Mr. Pugh read from it with
an accent so low-down that the very speech of the collector
of bad and doubtful debts who relates the episode came into
the Paris apartment. And there was Joyce on the sofa, smiling, while the voice of the strange tribe of Dubliners came
to him. "Ah! Ow! Don't be talking! I was blue mouldy for
the want of that pint. Declare to God I could hear it hit the
pit of my stomach with a click." When I laughed heartily at
the reading, Joyce said quickly, "I can read it in a more low-
down Dublin accent than that."


## VIII.  PADRAIC COLUM


Back in Paris in 1930, I went into the Shakespeare Head,
where Miss Beach received me as one of the confraternity.
When I asked about Joyce she laughed, as one about to mention a new quaintness. "Joyce wants you to do something for
him," she said. Of course she knew what it was, but as always

left the unfolding of it to Joyce himself. I gathered that whatever the project was, several of us were being mobilized for it. "Joyce operates like a general," I remarked to Ernest Hemingway, who was in the shop. "Like a general of the Jesuits," Hemingway said.

The present Joycean strategy, I learned, was directed toward furthering the interests of the tenor John Sullivan. Sullivan's name was on the Paris Opera House placards, and I had met him at Joyce's apartment on a festive occasion, at which he had sung—to Joyce's obvious delight. Though he was Irish, I had never heard Sullivan mention Ireland; indeed, I had hardly heard him say anything. He was a burly man, approaching fifty, apparently a long time in France: he never spoke anything but French in my hearing.

Everyone in the Joyce orbit, I quickly found out, had been brought to attention in the matter of Sullivan. But what part could I, so unlearned in music, perform? I awaited an order.

Joyce telephoned us soon after this. Were Mrs. Colum and I doing anything that evening? Nothing particular. Then would we go to the opera? He would be there and would meet us during the entr'acte. Wouldn't another evening do? No, Sullivan was singing and would not be singing again for some time. The opera was *William Tell*, and Arnold was Sullivan's great part. I was made to feel that anything we might do with ourselves in Paris that evening would be frivolous. And so—as Pepys would say—to the opera!

It was with some relief, that evening at the Opera House, that I found my attire permitted me to enter. Surrounded by busts of singers and composers, and by functionaries wearing chains that made them look like chancellors of universities and by others who had the appearance of high military and civic officials, I was made to realize that the prestige of the French opera, bound up, seemingly, with that of the French state, was not to be infringed upon.

Within the great hall we watched the arrival of ladies whose nationality we guessed at from their eyes or their fashion of wearing their wraps or jewels. They were all lovely and elegantly dressed on this spring evening. Naturally I thought of Owen Meredith's "Aux Italiens":

*And I turned, and looked. She was sitting there*
*In a dim box, over the stage; and dressed*
*In that muslin dress, with that full soft hair,*
*And the jasmine in her breast!*

*I was there: and she was there:*
*And the glittering horseshoe curved between:—*
*From my bride-betrothed, with her raven hair,*
*And her sumptuous, scornful mien.*

There were many beauties there that night with "sumptuous, scornful mien." But then the golden horseshoe with its tiers of seats grew still: there was not a cough, not a sniffle in that conclave. It was a well of stillness after the turmoil of the streets. The opera began. Sullivan, looking bulky in brown habiliments, came on.

Any story or play in which a man bends a bow and shoots an arrow is a good story or play, as far as I am concerned. William Tell shooting the apple off his son's head is a situation to hold any audience: it certainly held the audience in the Paris Opera House that evening.

At the entr'acte we met Joyce, with friends of his. He looked very festive. Sullivan was joining the party later for supper. We too were invited to join it, but my wife and I decided we would take beer and sausage by ourselves and go back to our hotel.

When, next day, I went to see Joyce at his apartment his talk from beginning to end was about Sullivan. The tenor was phenomenal in *William Tell*, Joyce maintained. Sometimes Joyce spoke impersonally, as if he had a statement prepared, and this was such an occasion. "There are eight hundred top notes in the tenor part in *William Tell*," he informed me I think, "including seventy in the very highest register between B flat and C sharp." My remarks about the opera must have seemed very feeble; I expect I gave the impression that all I had seen in it was the man with the bow in his hands. Joyce was instructive. He ranked Rossini among the very greatest composers, and he put *William Tell* with the great operas.

He became more personal. In *William Tell* he discerned the theme which he had worked out in *Ulysses*, the father's search for the son, the son's search for the father. The opera, he said, is about men's relation to the fatherland: into it comes the old patriot's relation to his son Arnold, and Arnold's love for Mathilda, whose father is the oppressor of the fatherland.

That Joyce had something in mind for me to do, in connection with all this about Sullivan and the opera, was manifest. But it was not until I was leaving that he told me what it was. "You have connections with a good many journals," he said. "I want you to write something about Sullivan." I told him I would. What and where were other questions.

I kept thinking of Ernest Hemingway's "Like a general of the Jesuits." I was amused to compare the tone of my conversation with Joyce over Sullivan with certain experiences I had had in connection with the fathers.

Staying in a certain town—there is no need to name it—I received repeated invitations to visit the editorial office of a review conducted by members of the Society of Jesus. The editor wished to discuss with me topics for possible articles. When I called at the office, the editor seated me—following a custom that some might call "Jesuitical"—where the light was on one face, mine, and not on his. Ultimately we reached a decision on the subject of my contribution. Father —— courteously accompanied me to the door. As we stood on the steps, he said, "Do you ever see any of our fellows now?" This referred, I knew, to men educated by the fathers whom I encountered abroad. Was this the primary reason I had been invited to the office? It might have been. Anyway, as we stood there, Father —— asked whether So-and-So and So-and-So were still "our fellows" in any approved fashion.

Joyce's procedure in asking me to help Sullivan was related to this. Not that it was indirect or tortuous; but his conversation with me had had, as had Father ——'s, a definite aim, and that aim had to be approached discreetly. There is a notion that Jesuit influence tends to heighten subtlety. It does if there is subtlety to heighten, but Joyce's mind would have been subtle even if he had been trained by behaviorists or pragmatists.

I think if one wanted to find evidence of Jesuit influence on Joyce, one might find it by looking to other sides of him—to his courtliness and reserve, for instance. Glenway Wescott, speaking of Joyce's manner and behavior, once said to me: "He seemed to belong to some secret nobility." This, perhaps, showed his training by the sixteenth-century order, Spanish by origin, which formed men to communicate with emirs and emperors, with shoguns and rajahs. Still, not many of those educated at Clongowes and Belvedere had Joyce's manner, or, as in the present case, his effectiveness in advancing some personal aim.

The slight push I was able to give Sullivan did eventuate in something. I wrote an article on the singer for the Dublin *Independent,* and afterward I, to my great exultation, had a note from Mr. Dempsey, formerly the Irish Minister in Paris, asking me to arrange a meeting between Sullivan and himself. I dashed 'round to Joyce's with the note. He took it as a boon and immediately invited Mr. Dempsey, and his wife, and myself and my wife, to dinner with him and Nora. We spent a very pleasant evening in the course of which Joyce purposefully told Mr. Dempsey about Sullivan's attainments.

Sometime after this the tenor was invited to sing at the inauguration of a church in Killarney. But the returned native wasn't at all impressed by his reception, and Madame Sullivan found Ireland very provincial, not to say barbarous.

Going to see Joyce before leaving Paris that spring, I found him in a downcast state. "A nice heavy piece of fat has fallen into the fire," he announced. Then I heard what was behind the alarming metaphor. An American newspaperman had been hanging around Joyce, hoping to get an interview with the famous writer. Joyce had availed himself of the correspondent's eagerness for his remarks to drop hints that Sullivan should be invited to sing at the Metropolitan. In the course of the interview Joyce mentioned casually that John McCormack had not done all he could for a certain other Irish singer. This had appeared in a New York paper as "John McCormack has no use for another Irish tenor," or something of the kind. Joyce, who valued his long-standing friendship with McCormack, was as disturbed as the novice who in his first published interview has blundered into some wildly slanderous statement. What was to be done to save Sullivan from reprisal?

I assumed the role of the traveled uncle. "Joyce," I said, "the hardest thing to find in New York is a morning paper in the afternoon. An item of that kind just won't stay in the public mind. You would have to hire a publicity man to keep the McCormack-Sullivan dissension alive." He came out of his dumps.

Nora came in just then, and I was warned not to let her know we had been on the subject of Sullivan: the household, I gathered, was beginning to be a bit tired of the name. But as I was taking my departure Joyce came to the door with me. Putting his hand on my shoulder, he said, "Keep your shoulder to the wheel about Sullivan." I promised him I would.

How persistent he was in his efforts to help the singer! I remember a later occasion, when my wife and I asked Joyce and Nora to a dinner we were having for some American friends. They came, although at the time Joyce was reluctant about meeting strangers, and his talk was almost solely about Sullivan. From what he said to me afterward I had to believe that his only interest in meeting our friends was that they might possibly be able to bring about an appearance for the singer in New York.

What was it made Sullivan of such concern to Joyce? There is no doubt he was prone to the *idée fixe*. He had conceived one in my own case, to a slight extent, believing—as I have said—that I knew the secret of the Dublin publisher's and printer's rejection of *Dubliners* and that there was some church or state reason for my keeping my mouth closed. And just as that notion was a fixture in his mind, so Sullivan and Sullivan's problems became an obsession with him.

Its source was plain enough. The Irish singer was fulfilling a part of Joyce's own desires. When Sullivan came on the stage at the Paris Opera, the Joyce who thought that the expression of the singer was the most immediate thing in art came on with him. But, for all his power and virtuosity, this singer was hardly known. So here was a project for the world-famous Joyce: to make Sullivan celebrated in Europe and

America, to get him acclaimed at Covent Garden and the Metropolitan.

Sullivan was getting on in years, however. What might be done would have to be done soon. Tenors after fifty are bad risks. Sullivan himself appeared unconcerned about all this. The humorous Stuart Gilbert said to me, "Joyce doesn't have to worry about Sullivan; he has a devoted wife, a charming mistress, and a girl in every town he sings in." Was Sullivan aware of the efforts Joyce was making on his behalf? Was he conscious of Joyce's anxiety about him? As I never heard Sullivan mention Joyce, I do not know.

## IX.  PADRAIC COLUM

To put James Joyce into a frame: as he approached fifty it struck me I should do this. I thought of a presentation that would be something of a portrait—his appearance at the time, his manner, items of his characteristic talk. The occasion I chose was a birthday celebration for Joyce and James Stephens, in 1931. Later I could not have done such a portrait; the settled conditions that invited it were dispelled. I give here some passages from the piece, which was published the next year in *The Dublin Magazine*.

*Slender, well-made, he holds himself very upright; he is tastefully dressed, and wears a ring in which is a large stone. The pupils of his eyes are enlarged because of successive operations, but his gaze is attentive and steady. There is a small tuft of beard on his chin. The flesh of his face has softness and color—the glow that a child's face has. A detail: his hands have now the softness, the sensitivity, of a man who has to depend a good deal on touch. All the lines of his face are fine; indeed his appearance is not only distinguished but winning. This appearance and his courtesy give him great dignity. Then when one takes note of his appearance one perceives that neither his head nor his forehead is large: the forehead*

*with three deep lines graven on it is narrow, the well-shaped
head is small. But head and forehead curve upward and out-
ward, giving a sense of fullness and resonance, each suggesting
instrumental amplitude. One can easily think of this head as
having correspondence with a musical instrument. The jaws
close to the chin make the face triangular; they too suggest
something in which there is sound. The abundant hair,
brushed backward, has lines in it that are like strings, like
iron-gray strings.*

*Noticeable, too, is his ease of movement. A musician who
knew him in Switzerland noted how easily he moved into the
dance. Probably it is because of this kind of articulation—
this gestic articulation—he possesses that he rates gesture as
the fundamental expression.*

*He is lying on a sofa when I come into his apartment. I
congratulate him on his gay attire: he has on a waistcoat on
which little dogs' heads are worked, and a very bright necktie.
He tells me that, feeling glum this morning, he had gone out
and bought himself a gay necktie. The waistcoat is a hunting
waistcoat; it was made fifty years or so ago by a grandmother,
whose portrait is on the wall. Other family portraits are beside
it, including one of Joyce's father painted by Patrick Tuohy,
and the arms and motto of the Joyce family—"Mors aut hon-
orabilis vita"—are displayed. . . .*

*Joyce tells me a story that James Stephens told him—a hu-
morous narrative of something that happened on his American tour. And after Joyce has told it bits of the story keep
coming into his mind, for he repeats lines and names out of
it, laughing again and again. The extravaganza which Stephens
related has the humor that appeals to Joyce. And Stephens'
treatment of some of the material gives him particular enjoyment—for instance, his reversing the name of the chief character, calling him sometimes "Reilly Wilson" and sometimes
"Wilson Reilly". . . . Such reversals have value in Joyce's
mind, for for him the comic situation, the comic character,
the comic phrase is the unsustained situation, character,
phrase. Leopold Bloom, diffuse and unsustained in his aspira-
tions and emotions, is a comic character, as against that man
of tension, Stephen Dedalus. As I consider this it seems to
me that the downward movement which puts men and women*

*on the levels on which we know them as comic characters and
which makes language absurd is, in Joyce's idea, an inevitable
reversal: it is as universal, it has as much of the Logos in
it, as the upward movement. And it is in their reversal that
Joyce is most ready to appreciate and express solemn things:
"Humpty Dumpty sat on a wall,/Humpty Dumpty got a
great fall,/All the King's horses and all the King's men,/
Couldn't put Humpty Dumpty together again"—the solemn
mystery of the Fall of Man is conveyed in this. Of all writers
of today, Joyce has probably the keenest appreciation of the
humor that arises out of ordinary life.*

*But I know that if I try to intellectualize his interests in
comedy of this kind, Joyce will ask me to talk to him of an
old woman selling apples on a bridge somewhere. He thinks
it a waste of time to discuss what are called "ideas." I once
asked him what a well-known sophisticated writer talks about
when with him. "Ideas," Joyce said, and his tone suggested he
was not very much entertained by the conversation. "I am
prepared to attempt to follow a discussion on the Procession
of the Holy Ghost," he remarked to me, "because an intellectual background has been created for the doctrine, but I
won't join a discussion on forms of government, nor on what
relations human beings have with the animal creation". . . .*

The birthday dinner for Joyce and Stephens, with which
most of the piece I wrote was concerned, was held in a restaurant. The Joyce family were all present, of course, and
Cynthia Stephens, as well as Miss Beach, John Sullivan, and
some other close friends. Joyce, who loved wine, had the waiter
bring a special kind which he recommended to us very earnestly: it was Clos de Saint Patrice (otherwise known as
Châteauneuf-du-Pape), from the part of France where Saint
Patrick sojourned after he had made his escape from captivity
in Ireland. Joyce would not have it that Saint Patrick was
born on the island of Britain—he was a Gaul, he insisted. He
noted how the Tannhäuser legend was attached, in its earliest
form, to Saint Patrick: when the saint crossed the river and
planted his staff, the blackthorn flowered, and *"les fleurs de
Saint Patrice,"* as the villagers called them, came out in mid-

winter. "He is the only saint a man can get drunk in honor of,"
Joyce said, in praise of Patrick as well as the wine.

The talk at dinner turned on other saints, but Joyce would
have none of them. He dismissed Saint Francis. He declared
he took little interest in Augustine. Aquinas, then, whose
aesthetic the young hero of *Portrait of the Artist* promoted?
Joyce would have none of the good Doctor either, or of Saint
Ignatius, despite his Jesuit training. The only saint he would
praise was Saint Patrick; him he vaunted above all the other
saints in the calendar. "He was modest and he was sincere,"
he said, and this was praise indeed from Joyce. And then he
added: "He waited too long to write his *Portrait of the Artist*"
—Joyce meant Saint Patrick's *Confession*.

That evening I had an instance of Joyce's genuine dismay
at anyone whom he knew possibly being involved in anything
violent. I had mentioned before this that the house I was
living in was being watched by the police; a Czarist general
had been kidnaped, and many Russians had apartments in
that building. Later I had thought the attic I had rented to
do some work in was being searched for papers. Joyce was
disturbed by this, and asked me at dinner if anything further
had happened. He seemed actually relieved when I said nothing had.

His aversion to aggressiveness, turbulence, violence of any
kind was quite deeply felt. "Birth and death are sufficiently
violent for me," he said. He was not only dismayed at the
thought of crime, he had no interest in it, and said he found
this a handicap in writing *Work in Progress*; a book that dealt
with the night life of humanity should, he felt, have some reference to crime in it, but he could not bring himself to put
any in.

After dinner we all went back to the Joyces' apartment,
where there was much jollity. Sullivan sang; Giorgio Joyce
sang; James Joyce sang. Joyce said to me: "John McCormack's
voice and mine are so similar in texture—as are my son's voice
and mine, in spite of the different pitch, and as are my own
voice and my father's—that more than once when a disc of
McCormack's has been on, the girl in the kitchen has thought
it was me."

Joyce was persuaded to do "Mollie Bloomagain," his famous

parody of a humorous Irish ballad, which he rendered with
gusto, and with the phrasing and intonations an old ballad
singer would have given it. And then he sang a tragic and
colorful country song I have never come across in any collection, nor heard anyone else sing. It is about a man who has
given his wife to a stranger—he may be from Fairyland, he
may be Death himself:

> I was going the road one fine day,
> Oh, the brown and the yellow ale!
> And I met with a man who was no right man.
> O love of my heart!
> And he said to me, "Will you lend me your love
> For a year and a day, for a year and a day?"
> Oh, the brown and the yellow ale,
> The brown and the yellow ale.

Those refrains in Joyce's voice had more loss in them than I
have ever heard in any other singer's. He once said to me,
"A voice is like a woman—you respond or you do not; its appeal is direct." He said this to show that what was sung tran-
scended in appeal everything that was written. His own voice
in the humorous and the sorrowful songs was unforgettable.

As Joyce neared fifty he appeared to me as sensitive and
enduring, not free from apprehensiveness, but with stoicism
enough to face what might be in the future. His vision had
been a problem since his schooldays. Constantly threatened
with loss of sight, he had undergone excruciating operations—
the year before he had had what I think was the ninth in a
series, and more were to come. The creative Joyce, the social
Joyce, was the person known to my wife and me, but when
I think of the menace of blindness, the suffering involved in
the treatment, the unclear world he was forced to live in, I
realize that Joyce had, literally, an obscure side. He would
speak of his fear of thunderstorms, of dogs or cats, but the
agonizing situations in his life he faced as manfully as anyone
could be expected to do.

My wife and I had been to dinner with the Joyces and some
of their closest friends on New Year's Eve, a few weeks before the birthday celebration I have described. That, too, had

been a very happy occasion. Eugene and Maria Jolas were
there, and Stuart and Moune Gilbert. At the end of dinner
Maria sang some operatic piece that Joyce had requested.
We spoke of poetry. Joyce liked the way I repeated verse, and
asked me to speak a poem—it was Blake's "Hear the Voice
of the Bard." As I repeated the compelling chant, as Joyce
remained perfectly still and the others fell into the mood, I
was really uplifted.

> *Hear the voice of the Bard!*
> *Who Present, Past, and Future, sees;*
> *Whose ears have heard*
> *The Holy Word*
> *That walked among the ancient trees,*
>
> *Calling the lapsed Soul,*
> *And weeping in the evening dew;*
> *That might control*
> *The starry pole,*
> *And fallen, fallen light renew!*
>
> *"O Earth, O Earth, return!*
> *Arise from out the dewy grass;*
> *Night is worn,*
> *And the morn*
> *Rises from the slumberous mass.*
>
> *"Turn away no more;*
> *Why wilt thou turn away?*
> *The starry floor,*
> *The watery shore,*
> *Is given thee till the break of day."*

That was an evening of good food, good wine, good companionship, good talk, music, and poetry. I cannot now be
sure of the interval between that and another dinner at
which my wife and I were again with Joyce and Nora. Again
a poem was said; it was Joyce who repeated it. This time the
poem was poignant, and it was said poignantly, for a poignant
experience was behind it. I will mention here only four lines
of it:

> *When hearts have once mingled,*
> *Love leaves the well-built nest;*
> *The weak one is singled*
> *To endure what he once possessed.*

"The weak one" was not Joyce; that made the poignancy of the expression.

## X.  MARY M. COLUM

Joyce had devoted friends: he was a reliable friend himself, and would help one with any old thing—with finding an apartment or a maid or a doctor, with planning a journey or picking out a hotel. If one of his friends was ill, he would shower him with attentions—principally bottles of wine. When we were in Paris he would telephone every day to find out how we were and how things were going with us. On the other side of it, Joyce expected a lot of attention from those he knew, and, on account of his eyes, a great deal of help.

His best friends were women, I heard him say. Let me start off the roll of his women friends with the names of Margaret Anderson and Jane Heap, who first published portions of *Ulysses* in America in their *Little Review*, and were put on trial for doing it. To get publication was necessary for Joyce at the time, and these understanding women got it for him. Then there was Maria Jolas, who helped him with his proofs when *Work in Progress* was being published in her husband's review, who sang to him and sang with him, and always gave him companionship that was both shrewd and warmhearted. (Years later she was to make his last days bearable and give him assurance that his daughter would be cared for.) There was Helen Kastor Fleischmann, who in 1930 married his son Giorgio, and who did so much to help and to entertain Joyce. And there were Sylvia Beach and Harriet Weaver, who did most for him as a writer—Miss Beach by undertaking the publication of *Ulysses* when no publisher in Europe would venture on it, and Miss Weaver by endowing him with a large sum of money.

Joyce had an odd capacity for acquiring money and patrons, and I can never imagine him as poor as many writers I have known. In Switzerland during World War I Mrs. McCormick, whom I mentioned earlier, gave him a thousand Swiss francs a month. Miss Weaver, who had once backed the feminist weekly *The New Freewoman*, and later *The Egoist*, in which some of Joyce's work appeared, first sent him five hundred francs a month and later gave him a sum of capital for investment—the amount was considerable, enough that, if he had been careful, he could have lived on it the rest of his life with ease. He was said to have had money from several other people. To Joyce this seemed normal: he was engaged in writing what he, as well as many others, believed to be great works of literature, and he thought it fitting that he should be supported while doing this by those who had the wherewithal to endow him. I know there are many stories told about his poverty, about his having to wear a long-tailed coat to hide the patches on his trousers when he was working in a bank in Rome. These stories are true, I am sure. Still, one cannot overlook his extravagance and the extravagance of his family.

What a pity that Miss Weaver did not, instead of giving him the money outright, settle on him a yearly income which he could not exceed. The lump sum had a bad effect on the whole family. None of them had much sense about money, and though they did not live in a very expensive apartment in Paris, they were extravagant about other things. Nora wore fashionable and costly clothes, generally from one of the grand couturiers, and beautiful hats. Joyce, after his day's work was over, liked to go to fine restaurants and eat, though sparingly, exquisite food, and drink, less sparingly, exquisite wine. For years he frequented Les Trianons, near the Gare Montparnasse; later it was Fouquet's—both were among the best restaurants in Paris in those days. Anything that deprived him of the pleasure of dining in such places, and of entertaining his friends there, was a calamity.

Joyce always behaved as though the money he had been given would last forever. I remember one festive dinner he

invited us to at Les Trianons, when Nora was away somewhere. Everyone drank a great deal of champagne, and Joyce,
departing in an expansive mood, presented each one of a
row of bowing waiters—none of whom had been assigned to
his table—with a hundred-franc note. I managed, with the
help of the proprietor or the head waiter, to collect these
hundred-franc notes, giving each waiter ten francs instead.
We took Joyce home and put him to bed, and I left the
hundred-franc bills I had retrieved in an envelope where he
would find them the next morning.

Miss Weaver once wrote Joyce that she knew he was spend-
ing money like a drunken sailor. It was after she told him
this that Joyce said to my husband, who had no money except
what he made by writing, "Morally, you are in a better position than I am."

When we first knew the Joyces in Paris, Sylvia Beach was
the person on whom Joyce most depended for all kinds of
help and for money. His day invariably began with telephon-
ing to or being telephoned from the Shakespeare Head, and
he or Giorgio or Lucia were in the shop nearly every day with
commissions for its owner. If any of the Joyce family needed
money they went to Miss Beach for it; the sums she advanced
them came, of course, out of royalties on the sales of *Ulysses*.

In time this arrangement led to bad feeling between the
Joyces and Miss Beach. Neither Nora nor Giorgio and Lucia
had any notion of what the financial returns on a published
book should be. They simply knew that many copies of *Ulysses* were being sold at a good price; they did not realize how
much of that money went for paper and printing, and for
overhead on the handling of copies. Joyce's family really
believed that Sylvia Beach was making an immense profit on
*Ulysses*, and that the Joyce household was not getting its
due. This led, I believe, to Joyce's asking Miss Beach for an
accounting, and perhaps to a claim that he was entitled to
have another outlet for *Ulysses*. At any rate, an antagonism
grew up between the Joyces and the Shakespeare Head, Joyce
being urged by Nora and Giorgio to take a strong line, and
Sylvia Beach being urged by her friend and partner, Adrienne

Monnier, to resist Joyce's growing encroachments on her energy and finances.

On Saint Patrick's Day—I think of 1931—Sylvia Beach and Adrienne Monnier got together with Joyce's special friends to give him a grand dinner in a restaurant, each guest contributing to the expense. Joyce said he would order for himself, and what the waiter brought him was a dish of lentils. Naturally the gesture made him quite conspicuous. The most amiable conclusion we could come to was that he was going in for one of his symbolic "correspondences." But it was certainly a bad way to behave on such an occasion; I have come to think he was childishly showing he was "out" with Sylvia Beach and Adrienne Monnier.

Perhaps it was at this time that Joyce made up that squib which I partly remember:

> *As I was going to Joyce Saint James,*
> *I met with seven extravagant dames,*
> *Every dame had a bee in her bonnet*
> *With bats from the belfry roosting upon it*
> . . . . . . . . . . . . . . . . . . . . . . . . . . . .
> *And, ah, I said, poor Saint James Joyce.*

But the extravagance was not all that of the "dames."

The breach widened more and more. Sylvia Beach had always spoken of him as "Mr. Joyce," as he had spoken of her as "Miss Beach," but now when she said "Mr. Joyce" there was a disengagement in her voice. On his side Joyce was beginning to have the look of a desperately driven man. I will always remember how, when he came to talk this matter over with us, he kept saying about a position he took, "Am I right or am I wrong?" He was earnest as only Joyce, with his intense expression and his pathetic eyes, could be earnest. Of course he wanted us to say he was right, but I could never bring myself to say that. I thought his separation from his first and greatest helper would be a tragic one. And I believe it was.

The actual break came, I think, over a letter Adrienne Monnier wrote Joyce. He showed it to me. It was written in French, of course, and I am not quoting it literally, but what it said in effect was this: "Gide said to me, 'What dedication

Monsieur Joyce has to his work! He never thinks about money.' 'On the contrary,' I said, 'Monsieur Joyce thinks all the time about money.'" Joyce was deeply wounded by this, because he was wounded in his dignity. There could never be friendliness again between him and the ladies of the rue de l'Odéon. But Joyce was a more sorrowful man after this estrangement. And with this resting on him he went on to what was really his great tragedy.

No doubt Joyce had what might be called a persecution complex; but this is not really surprising, for he actually was persecuted, I believe, in some of his relations with publishers and with those who had to do with getting his writing before the world—as witness the long struggle he had over the American publication of *Ulysses*. From the start Joyce had better luck with *Finnegans Wake*. As far back as the summer of 1931, when *Work in Progress* was several years from being finished, he had offers from American publishers for it which included advances of upward of three thousand dollars; in London, where he was staying that summer, he was offered four hundred pounds. Even these offers did not satisfy Joyce, however, for, as he wrote to my husband and me at that time, he was convinced that none of the publishers interested in *Work in Progress* knew "anything about the book."

Joyce's sense of being persecuted was not without basis for other reasons as well. He aroused jealousy and malevolence, and his personal affairs were often pried into publicly, and mean misinterpretations put on them. While the events that led to his estrangement from Sylvia Beach were going on, a copy of the American publication, the *Catholic World*, came to us in Paris. My husband, looking at the cover, noticed that the issue contained an article on Joyce by a Dublin man whom both he and Joyce knew. Seeing Joyce that day, my husband mentioned the article to him, though he himself had not yet read it. Joyce was interested in everything written about him, and particularly in anything written about him by a Dublin person, and immediately wanted to see the magazine.

I had read the article meanwhile, however, and was astonished that the enlightened editor of the *Catholic World*, Father Gillis, had published it. Not only did it denigrate Joyce as a writer; it also aimed at exposing his early family life as pretentious, sneering at family portraits and an occasional butler, and then it went on to place Nora in a lowlier milieu than she had been in. Anyone who knew Joyce would know that this was the sort of thing that would really hurt him, for it would humiliate him. I was determined that the article should never come under his eyes.

My husband told me that he had mentioned the article to Joyce, who wanted to see it. When he read it he, too, realized how much harm it would do Joyce, and we were both filled with consternation. The telephone rang. It was Joyce, wanting the *Catholic World*. "I left it behind me in some place I was in," I told him with what I hoped—but, knowing Joyce, had some uncertainty—was definiteness. There was a moment's silence, in which I knew he was making up his mind to circumvent my evasions. Then, "Giorgio is going 'round for it," he said.

I could no more have handed Joyce that magazine than I could have handed him a bowl of poison. Giorgio came. "My father wants to see the copy of the *Catholic World* you have." "I left it behind me some place." Giorgio paid no attention to the excuse and remained, evidently instructed not to leave without the magazine. After about an hour, apparently convinced he would not get it, he left.

Next day Joyce was in our apartment. "Mrs. Colum, I want you to give me the copy of the *Catholic World* that you have." "I haven't it, Joyce." "Tell me where you left it and I will have it traced." "I don't know where I left it." I fell back on every equivocation and finally had to say, "I won't give it to you, Joyce." "I'll stay here until you give it to me." And so, with that sad, resigned look on his face, he remained for a long time.

Then he left. We had a feeling that this petty business would mount and mount until it became an obsession with him. It did. It took him a long time to have his agents get him a copy of the magazine, but I never let him see the copy we had. Knowing how the sort of downgrading the article contained wasted his spirit, I made sure I would never be prevailed upon to let him see the magazine: I burned it.

## XI.  PADRAIC COLUM

Joyce and Nora were in London in 1930, and again in 1931. I remember a dinner there at which there were only the three of us as the friendliest session I ever had with Joyce. It seemed that his sense of persecution, often justified indeed, had recently been acute. Nora, indicating me, said, "Well, Jim, here's a friend." Joyce acquiesced openly and pleasantly.

Through a concatenation of circumstances I had three books out at the time; articles of mine were appearing in several magazines too; and there was an announcement—it remained an announcement—of a play of mine being done in New York. Referring to all this, Nora said, "I wish Jim would publish like you. He's in *transition,* but what good is that to us? He is the most famous writer in Europe now, and he could publish in any magazine." Joyce remained silent.

I was moved to say something on behalf of the productivity of the author of *Ulysses* and *Work in Progress.* "Do you remember," I said, "the fable that was in our schoolbooks in Ireland, in which all the animals discuss what they will do when the hounds appear? The hare speaks of all the doublings it will make, the fox of all the feints it will use. Then it comes to the cat. 'Alas,' the cat says, 'I have but one trick, and if that trick—'" here I remembered the way we used to say that line in class and gave it a childish whine—"'and if that trick fails me I am a lost cat.' Then the hounds appear. The hare, the fox, and whatever other animals there are around try their various tricks and are left in the lurch. The cat goes up a tree and remains out of danger. Moral: It is better to have one good trick than a dozen poor ones." I do not know if Nora was impressed. Joyce still said nothing, but he agreed, I think.

"Isn't it extraordinary," he said to me afterwards, "that none of my family read anything I write?" He must have mentioned that he said this to me and that I said it was hard on him, for Nora after that took occasion to tell me she often read and liked the *Anna Livia* episode in *Work in Progress*. But I recall that she once said, seriously, to my wife: "Don't you think Jim is making things very difficult for himself by writing the way he does?" And I don't believe Joyce's son or daughter knew much about his work either. He said to us one time, laughing, that either Giorgio or Lucia had asked him where they could find some examples of Irish humor—they seemed unaware of the great fund of humor in *Ulysses* and in their father's later work.

But now the Joyce household had acquired a new member —Helen Kastor Fleischmann, whom Giorgio Joyce had recently married—who did take some interest in Joyce's work. This young woman was the daughter of a well-known business family in New York, and had been married before. She was gay, high-spirited, and intelligent—an enlivening influence on Joyce. Helen typed installments of *Work in Progress* and discussed the book with a femininity that Joyce appreciated. "Amn't I the best secretary you ever had, Bappo?" she would say as she helped to prepare the unprecedented manuscript for publication.

Her presence brought friction into the house too, of course; there is an Irish country proverb to the effect that "No woman is good enough for another woman's son," and this was exemplified in Nora's attitude toward her son's wife. But Joyce seemed pleased by the marriage. "I hope they will give me a grandchild soon," he said—it was plain he was looking toward this as a fulfillment.

In December of 1931 Joyce's father, John Stanislaus Joyce, died in Dublin. He had done little, as a father, for his eldest son—in fact he had done nothing—but Joyce cherished his image and the memory he had of the musical, sporting, irresponsible, entertaining man. A few years after the publication of *Ulysses* Joyce had commissioned a Dublin artist, Patrick Tuohy, to paint a portrait of his father. There in the painting sat the elder Joyce, by then an old man, his face thrusting itself forward out of a green background, his eyes bulging and his mustache, the vestiges of a sport, waxed at the tips. A club man, one would say, whose self-will has gone with him all his life and now has left him cantankerous and easily exasperated.

There was a belief among Joyce's friends that he gave his father what he lived on. This was not the case, however. The old man lived on a realized insurance, with, perhaps, an old-age pension. Like many old men in Dublin who had some sort of position, he lived, not in a lodging house or a boarding-house, but with a family which, in those days, could let him have board and room for twenty-five or thirty shillings a week.

Not long after John Stanislaus' funeral I happened to be going from Paris to Dublin, and Joyce asked me to call on the family with whom his father had roomed. It was his hope, I think, that I would bring back some remembrances of the man on whom Simon Dedalus in *Portrait of the Artist* was based. I wrote to the head of this family when I got to Dublin, telling him I'd like to see him and talk about his late tenant. I had intended to visit him, so that I could get some impression of John Stanislaus' last surroundings, but instead he came to see me.

He was a nice young man who gave the impression that in his domicile the old man had been taken care of, but as he talked about him the emphasis was on the effort he and his wife had made to keep him decently. To him John Stanislaus Joyce was a battered, shabby old person who had come to live with them after some kind of a breakdown—either an accident such as befalls old men or a shock that had left him some-what astray. The young man knew that his tenant had meant something to the outside world, for a portrait painter had been in to put him on canvas and a newspaperman to interview him, but the John Stanislaus whom his son wanted to hear about had never existed for this young Dubliner.

So my report, when I got back to Paris, was disappointing, and I think I as its bearer was disappointing, too, to Joyce. For what had I brought back as a contribution to a noble elegiacal record? Here was I in an apartment that had on the wall Tuohy's "Portrait of a Dublin Gentleman" and other por-traits of men and women of his family. And I was making my report to one for whom the tradition of gentlemanliness was important. But what I had to tell was about an indigent old man who had come to spend his last days with people who knew nothing of the great times when he was a sport among Dublin sports, when his tenor notes were praised by an admired singer, and when there were people who knew he had hunted over every field in County Cork.

Joyce's fiftieth birthday came not long after that, in February of 1932, and he became a grandfather in the same month. The succession of death and birth was marked in his consciousness, and the poem "Ecce Puer," which he wrote on the birth of his grandson, is a poem, too, about the death of his father. "May love and mercy / Unclose his eyes" is his prayer for the child, but the last lines are, "O, father forsaken / Forgive your son!" "Mercy" and "forgive" are the telling words in the poem. With these words Joyce crosses into his fifties.

## XII.   MARY M. COLUM

My husband and I were called upon to be, in a surreptitious way, I am afraid, sponsors for Joyce's grandson.

Giorgio's American wife Helen had her own income, and so there had been no difficulties about the young people setting up their own establishment. When they had a child it was a great satisfaction to Joyce, and an uplift: he had a descendant to replace the father who had died just before. The grandson, named after Joyce's literary alter ego, Stephen Dedalus, also had his grandfather's first name—he was called Stephen James Joyce.

Giorgio Joyce had no religious affiliations, but Helen wanted Stephen to be baptized, and she chose my husband and me as godparents for him. The baptism had to be kept secret from Joyce, however, who was positively hostile to the Catholic Church.

It was a curious ceremony, with neither the father nor the mother of the child showing any familiarity with the religious rite. My husband's French was somewhat hazy, and though I had carefully schooled him in the proper answers to the questions, still he managed to get mixed up in the *Je renonce*'s and the *J'accepte*'s and the *oui*'s and the *non*'s, so that when the priest put the ritual questions as to whether, on behalf of the child, he renounced the Devil and all his works and pomp, he promptly answered *"Non."*

To crown it all, the priest asked graciously after the ceremony, *"Est-ce que l'enfant est le petit-fils de M. James Joyce, l'écrivain célèbre?"* We were all terrified lest the news of the ceremony get into the papers and all of us be berated, or worse, by Joyce. However, it seems that he did not hear of it until some years later, when I accidentally revealed it to him, and by then it made no difference to him one way or the other.

## PADRAIC COLUM

Joyce's abuse of the Church was apt to be what present-day Americans call "corny." It was mostly on the level of his "The Holy Office." On one occasion he said to me, "Léon was here yesterday, and he gave me a good dressing-down for what I said about the Pope the other evening." I remembered vaguely that Joyce had made some gibe about the Vatican and the Holy Ghost that his friend and helper, Paul Léon, a Russian Jew, had not been amused by. "What did he say to you?" I asked. The rebuke, coming from such a good friend, had evidently been felt by Joyce. "I said to him, 'You may have noticed that an Irish Catholic was present and he didn't raise any objection to what I said.' 'That may be,' Léon said, 'but you owe it to yourself to speak of dignified things in a dignified way.'" I thought at the time, Joyce must have been impressed by the criticism or he would not have confessed it to me. And his respect for his Jewish friend gained from it.

For all his railing against the Church, Catholic philosophy was the only system that meant anything to Joyce, and I often wondered whether there had not been a real question of his entering the Jesuit order by which he was trained, as there had been for Stephen in *Portrait of the Artist*. He spoke to me once of his decision in this matter, as if he really wanted me to know the truth. It was during a conversation when there were just the two of us in his apartment, and we had been talking of Dublin and of those small domestic details of Dublin family life, in his and my time, that for Joyce had such substantiality—the number of loaves and turnovers left for the household from the bakery van in the morning, the rattle of the milkman's can against the area railing. He mentioned then his early religious crisis and its negative outcome. "Mind you," he said, "it was not a question of belief. It was the question of celibacy. I knew I could not live the life of a celibate."

## MARY M. COLUM

In spite of his having broken with the Catholic faith, Joyce had not, as far as I could know, any of what are called Bohemian qualities or unconventionalities, that is if one leaves out of account his occasional heavy drinking. He was scrupulously moral and ethically above reproach. In spite of his visits to Nighttown in his student and post-student days in Dublin, he had fixed ideas of faithfulness in marriage, and nothing shocked him more than to hear that somebody he knew was committing adultery.

It is true that he had strong convictions about matrimony, maintaining it was strictly the affair of the two persons concerned, and not the business of Church or State. To hold such a view was like beating one's head against a stone wall, in Ireland, and must have been part of his reason for wanting to live on the Continent. Eventually he gave in on this question, and he and Nora had "the words of the tribe," as Mallarmé has it, said over them in a London registry office in 1931. In spite of all efforts to avoid publicity, the Joyces were photographed leaving the office where the ceremony was performed. The marriage was reported in the newspapers and scurvy journalists tried to interview him about his marriage, hoping he would say something that could go into headlines. Joyce was very upset. Hearing the name of one of the journalists, my husband said, "He is an Irish fellow." "I expected he would be," Joyce said with great bitterness.

I should like to add something more here regarding Joyce's relationship with or opposition to the Catholic Church. I remember that when I told him, during one of our reunions in Paris, of something Jacques Maritain had said—that Baudelaire's mind had a Catholic structure—he made fun of the statement. Actually, I have never known a mind so fundamentally Catholic in structure as Joyce's own, nor one on which the Church's ceremonies, symbols, and theological declarations had made such an impression. After he left Dublin I do not think he ever entered a church except for the music or some great traditional ceremony. And yet the structure was there: his whole mind showed the mental and moral training of the Church, and his esteem for many of its doctors and philosophers was greater than he expressed for other outstanding mentalities.

In 1941, when the news came that Joyce had died, some of his friends in New York wanted to have the customary Mass said for him. But every priest approached, even the Jesuits whose pupil he was and for whom he preserved great respect, refused on the grounds of Joyce's alienation from the Church. I will always remember that Father George Ford, the Catholic chaplain of Columbia, had the ordinary prayers said for Joyce in Corpus Christi Church.

## XIII.   PADRAIC COLUM

In the spring of 1932 we were living in the rue de Sevigné, in an apartment we had from Mrs. Eugene Jolas; the Joyces were living in Passy in a furnished flat. The distance between us prevented casual visits. The rue de Sevigné is not the most cheerful quarter in Paris, and neither was the Joyce's Passy flat the most cheerful place they had had in the city. Altogether it was a gloomy time. The carefree life of the year before was over; the depression in the United States was lowering royalties on books and making publishers chary of giving advances on new manuscripts. Now there were no festivities—or, as John Stanislaus Joyce would have said, no "jollifications."

Stuart and Moune Gilbert lived near us; we saw them frequently, and, as was usual with those in the orbit, the Joyces were often the subject of our conversation. It was from the Gilberts that we heard Joyce and Nora were having increasing anxieties about Lucia.

The girl had always been something of a problem. She and Giorgio had been born in Trieste and lived their formative years there; they spoke Italian to each other and to their parents, and had the look of Italian young people. But they had had to begin life all over again in Zurich during the war, when the Joyces were forced to go there, and then later, in Paris, there had been difficulties about getting them into schools that were crowded, at the time, with the children of displaced people. For all her Italian look, Lucia had grown into a French *jeune fille*; she had taken on the French values of the young girls she knew in Paris, and the question of a *dot* became all-important for her.

Lucia was distinctly a pretty girl, though not in an ordinary way. When we first knew her her eyes were a little crooked, which took nothing from the attractiveness of her face, though I believe it must have made her diffident. Later she had an operation to have her eyes normalized. She was talented in several ways, and had gone in for dress designing, and later for ballet dancing. But she wanted to be more in the world than she could be, living at home with her parents, and she wanted to marry. She complained that the young men who came to the house talked more to her father than they did to her. It seemed to me she was noticed, however: I remember a young Irish fellow whom my wife and I brought to a party at the Joyces', a party at which some of Lucia's young friends were present, saying as we left, "*Mademoiselle de la maison* is the most charming of the girls there."

The Gilberts told us that spring that Joyce had settled a dowry on Lucia, and that she was engaged, to a young man we knew as Alec.[1] He was a relative of Paul Léon, worked in a bank, and was quite eligible. But apparently the engagement did not solve all of Lucia's problems. We heard of her coming into a party and, having been offered a drink, saying that instead of a glass of sherry she would have half a cocktail,

[1] "Alec" was a more remarkable young man than this passing reference to him might indicate. His full name was Alexander M. Ponisowsry, and he was the brother-in-law of Paul Léon. He had a degree in economics from Cambridge University. It was he who introduced Joyce to Paul Léon, in 1928 when Joyce was taking lessons in Russian from him. Alec was arrested by the Nazis in April 1944 and, like Léon, he disappeared in some prison camp.

as that would enable her to face going home. This cannot all have been due to the gloominess of the Passy apartment.

Lucia had a particularly earnest, even formal, way of speaking, as if she had considered matters and had come to conclusions. But her speech, like everything about her, was deracinated. She would slip from English into French, and from French into Italian, in the course of going from one side of the room to the other. Her idioms were often wrong, as when she said, "She and I are in the same boots," speaking of another girl, an Irish girl she went about with, who was also engaged to marry a young man with a Russian name, and was having difficulties about it.

There was a feeling in the Joyce circle that Lucia would attain some equilibrium, if she did marry, and that her parents were doing all they could to clear the way for the marriage. But for all her seeming a normal, attractive young woman, there was something hesitant and solitary about Lucia, a sort of reflectiveness. "Lucia," she once said to me, explaining her name: "It means Light—like Paris, the City of Light, you know."

She came to see us sometimes that spring, and we were surprised at the violence with which she spoke against Joyce. Once when we suggested she come some place with us she said, "If anyone talks of my father I'll leave." When I mentioned to her some of the hardships Joyce had endured she said, "I saw him crying when he found he couldn't see to write." But she said it without any sympathy.

Joyce and Nora were planning to go to London that April, taking Lucia with them. They took leave of a host of friends, including the Jolases, the Gilberts, and the Colums. The day after the farewell I was in Miss Beach's shop. "They didn't get off," she informed me. I laughed; the Joyces' unpredictability had become a joke. There we were, believing that at that moment they were having tea in Piccadilly, and they hadn't got off.

But just as I laughed, Joyce stalked out of an inner room. He was on his dignity: my levity offended him. And then I learned that the reason for their not going was a serious one, and my humor pretty hurtful. Still keeping a detachment, he told me what had happened: they had been on the station

platform, all three of them, but when it came to boarding the
train Lucia refused to leave Paris, and showed such symptoms
of hysteria that they could not go without her, for it would
have meant leaving her by herself. There was nothing for Joyce
and Nora to do but take her back to the apartment. And Joyce
knew now they were faced with a real crisis.

Sometime after this Lucia came to stay with us in the rue
de Sevigné. Joyce had asked her where she would like to go,
since she seemed so unhappy at home, and she said she would
like to stay with Mollie, my wife. Mrs. Colum was fond of the
girl, and when Joyce spoke to us of Lucia's wish, my wife—
though she herself was in poor health at the time—asked Lucia
to come and live with us in the apartment.

I remember her coming in. It was night, and she stood looking out of a window. "That star," she said in her strange, reflective way, "means something." Pathetically she remained
there, looking out, for some time.

There was a notion among Joyce's friends that it would be
good for Lucia to have a routine job of some kind. A distinguished entomologist, an American, Dr. Howard, was living
nearby at the time, and he had mentioned that he wanted to
have someone familiar with English transcribe his notes for
him. We thought the job might suit Lucia, and Dr. Howard
agreed to try her out; one morning I took her to the entomologist's workroom. In the late afternoon she came back to the
apartment and, throwing herself down on a sofa, demanded,
"Is that the sort of work for me? Do you think it is? Why do I,
an artist, have to waste myself on that kind of work?" She
spoke as if she had a grievance. The kindly entomologist never
saw Lucia again.

My wife was afraid Lucia would do something to herself,
and slept in the same bed with her at night, pinning the girl's
nightdress to her own with a safety pin. It was a difficult time
for Mrs. Colum, who, we were shortly to find, was going to
have to have a dangerous operation. But she never ceased to
show Lucia fondness and attention.

Sunday came, and as I was going out to Mass, Lucia said
she would like to go with me. Joyce telephoned, while we were
gone, to ask about her. When he was told she was at Mass

he said, "Now I know she is mad." He did not know it, and it was the last thing he wanted to know, but Joyce often said things out of perversity.

## MARY M. COLUM

After Lucia came to stay with us, Joyce got a psychiatrist to come every morning to the apartment to visit her. We got Lucia to agree to see him by telling her he was treating me, and that it would help me for her to talk to him. So she and I sat together each morning on the sofa, I posing as the patient, while the psychiatrist flung questions at us. Sometimes I answered, sometimes she did. Lucia would describe what she considered my symptoms: *"Madame est très nerveuse,"* and the doctor would explain my supposed state by saying, *"Madame est artiste."* *"Mais, m'sieu,"* Lucia would then interject, *"c'est moi qui est artiste."* At intervals I would give some excuse and leave them alone together, and the conversation would go on.

Frankly, I had not much faith in the proceedings. The psychiatrist did not understand Lucia, and indeed I have never been able to comprehend how such a person, after a couple of interviews and without having known the patient previously, could come to any real conclusion about anyone's malady. I thought I knew more about Lucia's difficulty myself after having studied a while with Pierre Janet. I contradicted the psychiatrist flatly when he told me there was not much the matter with the girl, and that, whatever it was, she would soon get over it. Lucia's emotions were all in disorder, and to get them straight would take a long and very careful treatment. I believed she could get well only in new surroundings, where there was an atmosphere of affection and interest in her. Lucia believed my husband and I were giving her that, and had my own state of health not been so low I would have had her prolong her stay with us. And this not only for Lucia's own sake: when Joyce brought her to us and sat on the sofa beside her, when I saw his desperate, unhappy face, neither I nor any other human being could have refused aid. His face brightened as we welcomed the girl.

We made no difficulty about Lucia's going out with friends

after the psychiatrist's visits in the morning. While she was away from the apartment Joyce would telephone and often come in to talk to me about her. When I repeated one thing the psychiatrist had said—"Mademoiselle seems to have been hearing a good deal about sex"—Joyce said in a horrified tone, "She never heard about it from us." It is true that he was scrupulously correct in his speech: though he might, and probably did, talk freely to his men friends, I never heard him make a remark that would embarrass a nun.

We had been given instructions not to let Lucia go out in the evenings. However, Alec, her fiancé, was permitted to come and spend the evening with her in the apartment. One evening when he was coming Lucia said she would cook dinner for the four of us. So she put on an apron and went into the kitchen, where she helped me—or rather, I helped her—to get things ready. Alec came in, a young man rather too much on the correct side, I thought. Lucia served dinner, then took off her apron and sat at the table with us.

When the meal was finished she went into the room she and I shared, and came out again with her hat and coat on. "Where are you going, Lucia?" my husband asked. "Alec and I are going to the theater." Not a word from Alec, who stood as if ready to leave. "I have promised not to let you go out," my husband said. "Have I left my father's to be ordered about by you?" Lucia replied. Alec did not support her. "You are not going out," my husband said. "But I will go out," said Lucia.

Leaving Alec standing in the room, she opened the door and went out on the landing. My husband followed her. Down the flights of stairs they went, with "You are not to go," "I am going," being repeated all the way. But when they reached the house door poor Lucia said, "You win," and came back up.

In the meantime Alec had disappeared. When Lucia came in the apartment door she called him and then went in search of him. But Alec could not be found. Certainly it was something to bewilder the girl, for they had not met Alec on the stairs as they came back up. We were all at a loss to know how he had vanished. It was simple enough, I suppose: he knew the Jolas apartment and must have known the stairway up to the roof, and had gone out that way. But why he should have done this I do not know.

The whole scene was something to throw Lucia off her balance. Every time I think of it I am indignant. Why did my husband have to be so authoritarian?

I wanted to take care of Lucia. But now I was myself under the care of a doctor, Dr. Fontaine, who soon found reason to send me to that great surgeon Bergeret. And so, with her brother, I accompanied Lucia to a sanitarium. I did not tell her the truth about where we were going, though I hated more than anything to deceive someone who trusted me. But I was obeying orders, and did not know what else to do.

We entered the office of the director of the sanitarium, and as he began to talk to me, Lucia threw me a look of bewildered appeal which I can never forget. Later the director sent both of us upstairs to a room where Lucia was received by a pleasant nurse of her own age, for whom she took an immediate liking. The young nurse made her feel at ease, told Lucia she would be with her all the time, and her presence in the room made the good-by I had dreaded pass off more easily.

Between Lucia's going to the sanitarium and my going to a hospital for an operation, Joyce—restless and, I think, remorseful for not having seen his daughter's state of mind earlier— came 'round to our apartment every day. He was familiar with the place, since it was his friend's, Mrs. Jolas', and the grand piano that was there was one he had often sat before. When anything hit him hard, Joyce found relief in singing, and so, on these visits, he would play and sing, not to us but to himself. All the songs he chose—French or Italian pieces, or Irish ballads like the mysterious "The Brown and the Yellow Ale"—were sad. Then he would turn from the piano and talk about Lucia, with whose future he was now perpetually concerned.

Her malady grew tragically, and I think it affected Joyce more than anything that had happened previously in his life: perhaps it hastened his end. She came out of the sanitarium to which I had taken her, and we saw her the following winter in Nice. Later, however, she had to go back; during all the war years she was in a sanitarium in a part of France that was occupied by the Germans, and Joyce at his death was cut off from her, though he and Nora were able to get news of her from time to time.

I would not say that Joyce was a very good parent: he was too deeply immersed in his work. Sometimes he seemed barely conscious of the existence of the daughter he had written of as "my blueveined child." Obviously he had been delighted with the children when they were young; I heard him tell anecdotes of his son as a child with a parent's delighted interest. But the trouble with artists as parents is that their work claims too much from them—their intensity goes into it, and they are likely to be oblivious to their human commitments.

## XIV.  PADRAIC COLUM

The Joyces were in the south of France with Lucia, toward the end of 1932, and I had a few letters from Joyce from there. Here is the first:

*Hôtel Metropole, Nice*
*2. 10. 1932*

*Dear Colum:*

*Léon gave me a wrong address of yours. Anyhow I hope you got my card. Let me know how Mrs Colum goes on. These recoveries are very slow. By the way, did Dr Fontaine overlook anything in previous visits and was she taken by surprise? I ask on account of Lucia who, according to Dr F has or had nothing wrong with her. There is nothing mentally wrong with her now.*

*Thanks for the cheque. I wish now the poem did not appear in the* Criterion *for it is far too [illegible]. It should go into some simpler journal. But I cannot ask Eliot's people to send it back, can I? Or could I?*

*Yes, I received a couple of letters from Yeats and Shaw. But I did not answer. I shall do so in a few days. I have not been very well myself. In any case what have I to do with any such academy? I wish it all the success it wants.*

*Sincerely yours,*
*James Joyce*

The check for which Joyce thanked me was from the *New Republic*; I had sent his "Ecce Puer" to the editor. The poem was also accepted by Eliot for the *Criterion*, which evidently Joyce thought too sophisticated a publication for his lyrical response to the birth of his grandchild and the death of his father to appear in.

We decided to go to Nice for my wife's convalescence, and Nora secured rooms for us. On our first afternoon there, walking along the Avenue Victor Hugo, we came on the Joyces in front of their hotel, seated in deck chairs like any other arrivals off the Blue Train. Immediately we talked of Lucia. Giorgio and Helen were staying nearby, and Helen had taken Lucia out for a walk; according to Nora, the companionship of her sister-in-law was good for Lucia.

We had not seen the girl for months, and my wife and I wanted to have her with us for a while. But the Joyces seemed to think she should be left with her present entourage—or at any rate, they did not encourage us to ask her to stay with us. They were leaving Nice in a short time, and we saw them all together only that one time.

In his letter to me Joyce had mentioned hearing from Yeats and Shaw. This was about an Academy of Irish Letters that was being projected by Yeats, with Shaw as co-sponsor. They were proposing that Joyce become a foundation member of it. At our meeting in Nice he quoted to me the reply he had sent them. It was courteous; he declined, however, to associate himself officially with Irish letters.

I was surprised to hear he had made a friendly reference to Shaw in his reply—he was no admirer of G.B.S. (According to Arland Ussher, "Joyce" and "Shaw" are the same name— from "MacShoya.") "What can you say of a writer who has to write prefaces to explain his work?" Joyce had said to me once when Shaw's name came up. Had Joyce's downgrading of the other Irishman anything to do with Shaw's absurd comment on *Ulysses*, made in reply to a letter Sylvia Beach wrote him asking him to purchase a copy? The Dublin foulness, Shaw wrote—as if that were all there was in *Ulysses*—was what he had taken the trouble to get away from.

As for Yeats, Joyce had always regarded him as a great poet. He must have resented the fact if he knew of it that in that year, 1932, Yeats had passed over his work to say that a novel by a young Irish writer, Francis Stuart, was "perhaps more personally and beautifully written than any book of our generation."[1] But Yeats had spoken of *Ulysses* as a great work; I heard him say that *Remembrance of Things Past* and *Ulysses* were the great novels of the epoch. He put Joyce's before Proust's because of its "lonely intensity."

We stayed in Nice nearly a year—through winter, spring, summer, and early autumn—and so our contact with the Joyces, who were back in Paris, was at long range. I have a letter from Joyce dated a month after we saw them in Nice, however, from which it is clear that Lucia's condition had not stabilized as they, and we, had thought. Joyce was beginning to realize that it would exact more and more from him. The letter is short, on two pages, and unfortunately the second page of it is lost:

> Hôtel Lord Byron, Paris
> 2. XI. 1932

Dear Colum,

*I hope you are both well and that Mrs Colum continues to progress. Hughes wants your address. Most people here—the nurse, Helen, Mrs Jolas, Dr Codet and Dr Fontaine, think that Lucia's mind is deranged. Dr F gave me a long sermon a few days ago, saying that if I did what I did last July, i.e., took Lucia out of the doctor's hands she would probably have another and worse relapse and that I would repent all my life after. I went with Giorgio to see Codet and there was a long talk leading to nothing. The nurse is gone. Miss Moskos acts as a companion to Lucia, taking her around museums etc. We are still in the hotel as Miss Soneborg has said we should not go into a flat with Lucia. I took her books and alphabet* [here words are illegible]. *As for me, with all this cross-talk I know so little of what I am doing that last evening at 7.30 I lost the whole MS for* transition *in a taxi. I have been about all around Paris trying but cannot find it and have no copy. . . .*

[1] In *The Letters of* W. B. *Yeats.*

The books and alphabet referred to were Lucia's work: she was designing lettrines in the medieval style for Chaucer's Hymn to the Blessed Virgin. These illuminated initials, along with some she did for an edition of Joyce's *Pomes Penyeach*, and for another book of his, showed Lucia had a real artistic gift. Her lettering attracted a good deal of notice, including a mention by the art critic of the *Revue des deux Mondes*, who compared her designs to those of the Book of Kells.

With the exception of one, every name in Joyce's letter recalls a dolorous time. That one exception is "Hughes"—this was Herbert Hughes, a composer of our generation who hailed from Belfast and who had been for several years music critic for an important London daily.

In a certain Irish coterie Hughes was known as "Paudeen." A Dublin woman said of him, "Paudeen should wear a stock," and this was a neat way of imaging him, for, round-faced, wearing spectacles, and with a smile that seemed to come from relish of some naughty thought he had had, Herbert Hughes brought some eighteenth-century portrait to life.

My association with him went back to youthful days. We had collaborated in collections of Irish folk songs, he getting down the music and I building up the song from fragments attached to the tune. Naturally he was attracted to Joyce's songs. What brought him to Paris at this stage was the project, now realized, of having the leading musicians of Europe make settings of *Chamber Music* and *Pomes Penyeach*. These words with music came to be published, in 1933, in a handsome volume, *The Joyce Book*, edited by Hughes.

Joyce delighted in having a musician by him. And Paudeen was also an entertaining fellow. He would talk in a ponderously knowing way about the great musicians, and then become the boy from Belfast, putting on the clipped Ulster accent and using the Ulster idiom ("Do you see yon cuttie wi' the weans?"). He loved to tell those stories, the point of which is the Ulster man's or woman's combativeness, expressed very succinctly, or else his or her unconsciousness of any milieu except—well, let us say, Tandragee. Hughes and James Stephens would have made a notable team; Stephens, however, was far superior in imaginative energy. "Paudeen" was really a good mimic, and the stock characters of the Belfast comedy (in those days the mayor headed the cast) were rendered by him in their characteristic humors. "That's not a bad wee dog ye're holdin'," the mayor says to the son whom he meets on the street. "It's not intended to be a bad wee dog."

Joyce had taken to Hughes' stories and expressions just as he had taken, earlier, to Stephens'. One of the former rates a line in *Finnegans Wake*. Hughes told a story of the Mayoress of Belfast showing visitors a line of portraits and announcing, as she indicates her husband's, "Oil painted by hand." Joyce was then writing H.C.E.'s glorification of his municipal career, and his comic treatment of the gallery of mayoral portraits assembled arose out of the bit of comedy Hughes related with North of Ireland tang. Here is the echo: "we had our lewd mayers and our lairdie meiresses kiotowing and smuling full-face on us out of their framous latenesses, oilclothed over for cohabitation and allpointed by Hind."

Hughes' name in Joyce's letter provides a transition between the lively times and the subdued ones. It seems to me as I look back, that halcyon days and ambrosial nights had, after the sessions with Hughes, no recurrence.

## XV.  PADRAIC COLUM

We were not to see the Joyces for a long time. My wife got well in Nice, and in the autumn of 1933 she received an offer from the *Forum* to conduct its literary section. We left for the United States from a Mediterranean port.

It was nearly five years before we were in Paris again. Back there in the summer of 1938 we felt an anxious awareness of Hitler on one side and Mussolini on the other. And one evening, returning from a visit in the country, we saw that Paris was no longer the City of Light. The festive times were over. The dimness in the streets made us feel the dispiritedness of the citizens. Our concierge gave us a list of things we were to take to the basement with us in case of bombardment, and

the municipality was advising people who did not have to stay
in the city to go elsewhere during the emergency. Simple people were asking, "Where is Czechoslovakia? Do we have to
go to war for people there?"

To Joyce, disturbed by thunderstorms and timid of dogs,
the menace of war must have been hardly endurable. He and
Nora decided to leave Paris, to go to a place where Lucia
could be looked after. Before their departure it was some
relaxation for Joyce to go for walks with me.

What did we talk of? Lucia. Her condition, which had
worsened year by year, was beginning to take on the dimen-
sions of a life's disaster. I could see some remorse in Joyce's
present attentiveness to the girl.

He put some of the blame for her state on Nora. She had
not nursed Lucia as a baby, and he had had to get his young
sister to come and live with them in Trieste so that the children would be taken care of. Joyce often had something to
say about Nora's bad housekeeping, putting it down to her
stupid upbringing in a convent in Galway. This criticism of
her, however, did not imply any separation of interests: he
remained devoted to Nora.

His feeling about Lucia was more intense than Nora's was;
behind it, I felt, was a realization of having failed to meet the
claims of a growing child, claims that suddenly, in the middle
of his preoccupation with very different interests, had fallen
due. As we walked together, Joyce sometimes silent, sometimes conversing, I realized how tragically lonely great fame
can leave a man.

But I also remember oddities of discourse on these promenades. Why did Joyce have to be abusive about nuns? Why
did he think that nuns ranked with tailors in a sort of nullity?
He reminded me: "They have no office in the Church. They
can't even assist at Mass like altar boys." He did not mention
that one of his sisters was a nun. She was in a convent in New
Zealand, and from what I heard from one who had visited her,
she had an affection for James, for she kept as a relic the
surplice he wore as a boy when he served at Mass. (The mention of Joyce as an acolyte reminds me that no exegete has
noticed in his prose the cadences of the Latin responses to the
celebrant, broken by the ringing of a bell in an unfilled

chapel.) A priest among passers-by drew a favorable comment from Joyce on the garb of French priests. They wore soft hats. "If somebody would kidnap the silk hats of the priests in Ireland, wouldn't that be a gain for the Church?" he remarked.

## MARY M. COLUM

I remember an incident from this visit that was a reminder of happier times. Joyce still liked to dine in places where there were lively crowds; he went regularly now to Fouquet's, in the Champs Elysées, the haunt of celebrities of all kinds. He could not, with his poor vision, see many of the diners, but he liked to be told who they were.

Once, while waiting for a table in this place, we sat on a bench next to a man in tweeds and a blonde, rather tired-looking woman, without make-up, in a black suit. The woman looked so familiar I began to wonder where I had seen her before. Nora enlightened me: "You have seen her in the cinema; she's Marlene Dietrich."

I turned to the woman impulsively and asked, "Are you Madame Dietrich?" She answered, not unpleasantly, "And who, madame, are you?" I responded that I did a little writing. "Oh, then you will like to meet Monsieur Remarque," she said, introducing the tweed-clad man with her. In return I introduced the man at my side: "Monsieur James Joyce."

The effect was electrical. I had not imagined that such a writer would be of interest to a movie star, but both Miss Dietrich and, more naturally, the novelist with her were excited at the encounter and were loath to leave when their table was announced. The observant waiter gave us a table next to theirs, so the conversation was continued for a time. "I saw you," Joyce said to the star, as if he were speaking of some event far back in history, "in *L'Ange bleu*." "Then, monsieur," Miss Dietrich replied, "you saw the best of me."

Joyce was amused by it all. "I thought the years when I was a lion were over," he said, smiling, but with a kind of melancholy. He was at the last lap of *Finnegans Wake,* and, as usual, was mobilizing helpers. He and Nora left Paris shortly after this; we had not seen much of them.

## PADRAIC COLUM

Then came Munich, and a shamefaced relief was evident, at least at first, among the sojourners in Paris. The Joyces came back to the city. When Joyce telephoned me he mentioned the settlement. "Give him Europe!" he said angrily.

"Peace in our time"—but one saw more and more sad-looking people in the Paris streets: refugees from Hitler. Joyce had become concerned about a Jewish family the head of which was Edmund Brauchbar, who had been a pupil of his in Zurich years before. Herr Brauchbar was in Paris trying desperately to arrange places of refuge for relatives who were in danger spots in Germany or Austria. Some had been placed in Sweden, some in England. The family included many members, and Herr Brauchbar, a rich manufacturer, seemed ready to spend his entire fortune to procure sanctuaries for all these people.

He had been helpful to the Joyces in Switzerland, and when he asked Joyce for help in settling a cousin, a brother-in-law, or a nephew in this place or that where he had some influence, Joyce was ready to give it. Herr Brauchbar thought Ireland could provide a temporary refuge for one of the young men; Joyce asked me to write to someone in the Ministry on this person's behalf.

What a change had come over Europe in a few years! Here was a young man with nothing whatever against him who wanted to take up residence in a country. All he would have had to do, a little while before, would have been to buy passage and go there. Now it was a question of government procedure. I wrote to the Minister of Justice, telling him that this young man would not oust anyone from a job, that he would not be a charge on anybody, and that, as long as he was in the country, he would have an adequate income from relatives. The reply I had from the Minister was formal. It said that a residence permit could not be given—I have forgotten what reason was stated—to the person about whom I had written.

It happened that Herr Brauchbar came to our apartment the afternoon of the day I received this reply. Our conversation still remains in my mind. The elderly, successful, well-dressed man of the world, obviously used to telling people where to go and what to do, broke down and wept. "Kill us," he cried, "but don't deny us everything."

I knew that the matter could not be allowed to rest there. When I telephoned to tell Joyce of the reply I had had he said indignantly, "Who is the fellow who refuses residence to people of that kind?" Then he said, "You didn't put the matter strongly enough. Write to the man again."

I did. I made my letter eloquent. I reminded the Minister of Justice how often Irish people had to seek refuge, and with what gratitude they looked on countries that gave them a place. Immediately, to my own and Joyce's relief, the Minister sent permission to Herr Brauchbar's relative to take up residence in the country. It only showed what a strange world we had come into, that there should have been any question about it.

My wife and I made a trip to Germany about this time, where we saw firsthand how the world had changed. As we traveled on trains there were continual halts at which young men in uniform jumped on and off. In entertainment places in Munich we saw a young generation trying hard to conceal its shabbiness; and the sculptured group representing the heroes of the Munich *Putsch*, how top-heavy it seemed! And those nice Bavarian maids who began their address with "*Gruss Gott*," all hesitated and then said hurriedly, "*Heil Hitler!*" Everywhere we felt the giddiness one experiences when the name given does not correspond to the thing seen.

Back in Paris, we dined with the Joyces—the last dinner, as it turned out, that we were to have together, Joyce and Nora, my wife and myself. I think of that meal as being grave in tenor. The talk, naturally enough, was of public affairs and of Lucia. For a man who talked of politics with reluctance, Joyce's stand on the European crisis was impressive. He spoke in a measured way, condemning Mussolini's Italy for putting the squeeze on France, stating his absolute confidence in the French army. France, because it was rational, was for him Europe's highest civilization. "Where else," he asked, "can you go out to dinner and have a cardinal on one side of you and a commissar on the other?"

Of his wife's and his own personal problem, Lucia, Joyce

spoke with surprising objectivity. He had always decried sentimentality, but now he talked about both Lucia and Giorgio in an oddly appraising way. Giorgio had made a good marriage; Lucia's inclinations had been toward young men who did not regard her as a good match. "Jane Austen named my children," Joyce said, "—Sense and Sensibility." As he continued to speak of Lucia in a rather detached way, Nora protested that he had never really known his daughter. "Allow me to say that I was present at her conception," he rejoined. I had reason to know that his objectivity had been reached through great stress, and could not be persisted in.

I remember that there was a humorous passage in the somewhat grave proceedings, however. In Nice five years before, my wife and I had taken much stock of two figures who were to be seen around the town—they were partners, one an ascetic blind man who played a violin in the streets, and the other a follower, who accompanied him around, collected the donations, guided him here and there, and took him to bistro and lavatory. My wife had maintained the partners were replicas of Joyce and myself. Once or twice we saw one of them without the other. "Where is your friend?" my wife asked the follower, when we saw him by himself. "M'sieu," he responded, as if speaking of a celebrity, "rests himself." On another occasion we found the blind violinist seated alone in a little park. We asked him, after a time, where his companion was. "Eh? Who? . . . Ah, le vieux!" The blind man laughed, or rather, chuckled, apparently at the notion that anyone should expect him to know the whereabouts of his hanger-on. Joyce enjoyed the story and kept laughing over it. "Which was 'M'sieu' and which was 'le vieux,' Colum or Joyce?" And so the evening had its genial side.

Joyce was able to distract his wife's attention while he got the waiter to bring him another bottle of white wine. I conducted him downstairs and had him back and at the table in time to finish his wine before Nora, who had also retired, reappeared. She found him standing before the bowing waiters, whom as usual he had tipped extravagantly.

We were obliged soon afterward to leave Paris for New York. Joyce, in spite of many troubles, was on the last pages of what would be entitled Finnegans Wake. His good friends

and helpers were around him as always, but no one could
avoid feeling the anxiety of the time.

We had boarded the boat train when, looking out of the
window, we saw Joyce and Nora coming along the platform.
They had come to see us off. For ten minutes the four of us
were together. We talked to them about being back in a year,
about remembrances to friends, about the reception that
would be accorded the long-worked-on book. I knew all the
time we were talking that for Joyce this was a real separation.
In Europe a feeling of desperation was rising; our friends had
a personal problem as well, and one of them was learning that
it was insoluble. We were going from a continent filled with
misgivings and dangers to a continent where violence and
stupidity were not threatening the people, and Joyce said this
in his well-wishing, it made his well-wishing the more earnest.
He was sad, he was lonely, he was resigned; he was here out of
an old friendship. It was a very different leave-taking from
others we had had from him in the earlier Paris years, when
he was the genial Dublin man, happy with family and friends.

"Good-by, Joyce! Luck to *Finnegans Wake*," we called. As
the train began to move, Joyce, stumbling on a bit, said to my
wife, "We don't want you to go, but anyhow you'll be safe
in America."

## XVI.   MARY M. COLUM

I received a letter from Joyce in April 1940 from St.
Gérand-le-Puy, Allier, in Vichy France, where I had written
to him with regard to Herbert Gorman's biography of him,
just then published and which I had reviewed. The letter[1]
contained an amusing paragraph describing the response of
one member of Joyce's public to a portion of *Finnegans Wake*
—a response that was perhaps an ironic echo of that being
accorded the book itself, published the year before:

[1] Published in *The Letters of James Joyce*, edited by Stuart Gilbert
(New York, 1957).

*I am not sure whether you took Italian at the R.U.I. [Royal University of Ireland]. Anyhow the Italian translation I made of Anna Livia (incomplete) was published in* Prospettive *(15 Feb 1940, Rome) together with several articles about the book. If there is a good Italian bookshop in New York you might find a copy. It had an amazing sequel. The next number (15 March) contains a photograph of the Italian Minister of Education, Signor Giuseppe Bottai, apparently sent to the editor by him. It purports to be a photograph taken after a reading of the number devoted to my "prose". His Excellency is represented as seated at a table with one hand clasping his forehead, his eyes closed and an expression of exhausted bewilderment on his face. He has written a despairing ejaculation on the side of the photograph. Several years ago when he was governor of Rome he wrote to me inviting me to be a guest of honor at some banquet or function—I forget now what it was. I replied thanking him but did not go. I did not even send the efficient and witty Stephens to replace me as I had done in the case of an invitation to [Florence?] by the mayor some years before. He was not a complete success as he did not know any Italian. However the pained look in the photograph will soon give place to the first of many similar [?smiles].*

This letter is the last I have from him. He died in January of 1941, in Zurich.

Some years after the war, my husband and I received a touching letter from Nora Joyce, acknowledging some funds we had raised for her. The letter is undated; it was written from Zurich some time before she went into the hospital where she died in 1951.

> *Hotel Neptun*
> *Seefeldstrasse 15*
> *Zurich*

*Dear Padraic and Molly,*
*I really don't know how to thank you and your friends for your very kind gesture in sending me two remittances of 50 and 40 dollars. You can't imagine what a help it is for me to receive some financial aid as I have not received any money from England for seven months except £20. Luckily my*

solicitor was able to arrange that I get some of the royalties direct from America. It is very difficult for me because I have to support Giorgio who has absolutely not a penny of his own and can't get work here. I am so glad that you saw Stephen [the Joyces' grandson] and find him such a fine boy. Giorgio did all he could for him while he was here.

I am afraid I shall sooner or later have to sell my manuscript of "Chamber Music" written in Dublin in the year 1909 and dedicated to me; it is written on parchment and bound in cream coloured leather with the Joyce crest on one side of the cover and our initials on the other side. If you know anybody who you think will be interested in buying such a work would you kindly let me know.

Please convey my best thanks also to Mr Sweeney and Mr Healy for the very welcome financial help.

With warmest thanks to you and Molly and with kind regards,

Sincerely yours,
Nora Joyce